DUCHESS BAKE SHOP

DUCHESS

BAKE SHOP

by Giselle Courteau

Design, Layout & Art Direction · Sarah Hervieux
Editor · Mona-Lynn Courteau
Recipe Revision & Testing · Jacob Pelletier
Props & Food Stylist · Sarah Ares
Photography · Amanda Gallant of AG Photography
Procedure Photography · Aaron Pederson of 3Ten Photography
Sales, Marketing & Revision · Garner Beggs

Duchess Bake Shop
10720-124th Street, Edmonton, Alberta T5M 0H1
www.duchessbakeshop.com | info@duchessbakeshop.com

Provisions by Duchess
10720-124th Street, Edmonton, Alberta T5M 0H1
www.duchessprovisions.com | info@duchessprovisions.com

ISBN 978-0-9939012-0-1
Legal deposit—Library and Archives Canada, 2014

Printed and bound in Canada

Published in Canada in 2014 by Duchess Bake Shop.
Distributed in Canada by Duchess Bake Shop.

First published—October 2014
2nd edition—December 2014

Callebaut and Cacao Barry are registered trademarks of Barry Callebaut A.G.;
Nutella is a registered trademark of Ferrero S.P.A.; Valrhona is a registered
trademark of Valrhona.

TABLE *of* CONTENTS

———

a day at DUCHESS

EARLY ON A SATURDAY MORNING, long before the sun rises, the neighbourhood around Duchess Bake Shop is quiet and calm. Inside the kitchen, however, the scene is very different, with bakers hard at work on a myriad of tasks: kneading dough, chopping chocolate, filling éclairs, shaping tarts. Every day starts early at the bakery, but on a Saturday morning, the busiest day of the week, the pace in the kitchen is in overdrive. Hands are flying and all eyes are on the clock as opening time nears.

There is a long list of tasks to accomplish in the few short hours before the doors open. Dozens of cakes are lined up on the maple-topped workstations waiting to be covered in chocolate or draped in marzipan. Brioches and croissants are proofed, macarons are filled, scones are mixed... the list seems endless. There is a long line of trays waiting for their turn in the hard-working ovens. As products are finished they are organized and arranged on rolling racks ready to be wheeled out to the front. The orders for the day have been written out on a large white-board and begin to be filled in order of pick-up time, and soon a small mountain of neatly labelled white boxes has grown.

At 9:00 am, the front staff begin to arrive to prepare the café area. Silver trays are loaded up with piles of still-warm croissants, scones, galettes, brownies, and cookies and put out in the glass display cases. The front coolers are turned on and filled with the day's assortment of tarts, cakes, and a veritable rainbow of macarons, the shop's specialty. The espresso machine is warmed up and hundreds of cake boxes are readied for the day to come.

After a brief meeting to make announcements and go over changes in the product line, the doors are opened to let in the line-up of people who have been patiently waiting outside. The first hour will see over 300 people come through the doors. Shots of espresso are pulled as fast as the two baristas can manage while sandwiches, quiches, and salads are prepared to order in the back. The front staff won't have the chance to catch their breath until well into the afternoon.

After opening, the kitchen switches modes and begins to prepare for the next day. Hundreds of lemons and limes are juiced and zested, dry ingredients measured out in ranks of steel bowls, macaron shells piped and baked, deliveries of ingredients sorted and stored. At 1:00 pm additional bakers arrive. They will be there until well after the front has closed to ensure that the display cases will again be full the next morning. The last to leave are the cleaners, and then the kitchen goes dark for a few short hours until the bakers come back the next morning and the cycle begins again.

· JACOB PELLETIER, GISELLE COURTEAU & GARNER BEGGS ·

THE DUCHESS STORY

THE IDEA FOR DUCHESS was born in the heart of Tokyo in the summer of 2007. Giselle and I had been living in Japan teaching English for two years and were trying to figure out what we would do when we eventually returned to Canada. I had long thought of having a small café and Giselle had always wanted to open a bake shop and so, after some long discussions, we decided to try to make those dreams a reality.

While Giselle had long been obsessed with macarons, I was very skeptical. Why were they so expensive? Why were there always lines of people waiting to buy them? It only took a single bite of Ladurée's salted caramel macaron for me to see the light. From there, it took Giselle two more years of constant research and testing to perfect her own version of them. That research included countless trips to the vast number of high-end pastry shops in Tokyo. We would spend our weekends walking from shop to shop comparing products, ambience, uniforms, and service styles. Slowly the full concept of what Duchess Bake Shop would be took shape. At its heart was a firm commitment to putting quality first. You can't fake good-quality ingredients and we could always tell if a bakery was using artificial flavours or premixed fillings. We vowed that no matter what, we would always start with natural ingredients of the highest quality and in as raw a state as possible.

We finally left Tokyo and returned to Edmonton in April of 2009. In October, only six months later, Duchess Bake Shop opened its doors in a small 1,500-square-foot space on 124th Street in the heart of Edmonton, with seating for just ten customers. The construction had been done on a shoestring budget with the aid of money lent by family and numerous hours of work donated by friends and family, often in long, gruelling 24-hour marathons. We really weren't ready the day we opened, but our funds were depleted and there wasn't much of a choice. I vividly remember peeling the wrapping off the cash register mere minutes before opening and standing there with my good friend trying to figure out how to program it as the first curious customers wandered in.

In so many ways we were woefully ill-prepared for the realities of owning our own business. Thankfully, in that first week Jacob Pelletier, who was destined to become the third partner in the venture, came into the shop freshly back from working in England and curious to see what this new bakery in town was all about. He started work that very day, and without his tremendous ability and drive we might not have pulled through.

The next year was a complete blur. Ignorance is bliss, as they say, and I often wonder whether if we had known how hard it was going to be we would have gone forward with it. All of us were working around the clock grabbing an hour of sleep here and there. We started taking taxis to work after falling asleep one too many times at red lights. Thanks to the tremendous support of the community around us, we grew quickly—very quickly. We couldn't make nearly enough to satisfy demand. The staff size doubled and then it doubled again. The books were a mess. Personal relationships

CONTINUED

started to fray and then fell apart under the load of stress and exhaustion. The idea of having even a single day off was a distant memory as the months of 18-hour working days went by. However, every day we got a bit better at it. The kitchen would figure out a new way to streamline production, the front would try a new way of handling orders or making coffee. Bit by bit we found our feet and started to work out the kinks and improve our efficiency and the quality of our products.

And then, suddenly, the prospect of expansion came upon us. The neighbour in our building was moving out and, although we still hadn't caught our breaths, we had to seize the opportunity. So just over a year from opening we took on the challenge of tripling the size of the business and restructuring. Jacob came on board as a partner with Giselle and I and we used our growing reputation to secure financing. I put on my overalls again and, with tremendous help from friends and family, dug into a new construction project. There were some very tense moments financially with payrolls made with mere cents to spare, but after four months of renovations we had our new café space and kitchen facilities complete with a proper espresso machine, double the display space, four times the seating, and room for our rapidly expanding Duchess family.

Originally three or four servers could handle the front on a busy Saturday and we had four bakers. Today we have around 60 employees including 16 full-time chefs working in the kitchen. We take up 4,500 square feet of space and have opened up Provisions by Duchess in our original space next door selling cookbooks, baking tools, and ingredients. Things continue to evolve, change, and grow, and that's exactly how we like it. Through it all we've managed to adhere to our dedication to providing the best possible quality products and service to the public. It's been hands-down the most challenging, exhausting, and draining thing I've ever done, but also the most rewarding and exhilarating.

Today, Duchess is a modern family and we are honoured to work alongside each other every day. We've been lucky enough to become a valued part of our community and of our city and to push and expand people's expectations of what quality food should be. We are all eternally grateful for the tremendous support of the community around us and our friends and family without whom this never would have been possible.

Garner Beggs

a note for the HOME BAKER

I AM FIRST AND FOREMOST A HOME BAKER. Since I was a little girl I've loved baking and making pastries. My mother, despite working full time, was one of those supermoms who made everything from scratch. Growing up, I often wanted the pre-packaged snacks and desserts that the other kids had in their lunchboxes. When I begged for them at the grocery store, she would tell me that if I wanted those things I should just make them myself. And so, from a young age I was driven to the kitchen to bake from scratch to satisfy my insatiable sweet tooth. At the time, I didn't understand that not only was my mother instilling in me a passion for baking, she was also giving me an even greater gift: real food made with real ingredients.

I'm a self-taught baker. I've never had any extended formal training and don't have natural talent in the kitchen, but I'm passionate about baking and pastry. I've taught myself a lot by reading books and scouring the internet, but also through plenty of trial and error —persevering despite my often disastrous results. Since opening Duchess my skill set has grown immensely. I have learned from not only Jacob, our co-owner and a classically trained pastry chef, but also all the other amazing chefs I've had the pleasure of working with in our kitchen.

Pastry and desserts are for celebrating, spending time with family and friends, and treating ourselves. Have fun with it and don't take it all too seriously. If you don't succeed on your first try, don't give up: every time you make a recipe, you'll learn something new to improve it next time. Allow yourself the freedom to make mistakes and be sure to take pride in your end result, whether it looks like the picture or not.

Duchess Bake Shop is the perfect balance between home baking and high-end French pastries. We make everything from scratch using real ingredients. There are no secrets to what we do and no magic tricks to making our final product, and that's why we wanted to write this book. I hope it helps you gain confidence in the kitchen and inspires you to try new ideas of your own.

Giselle Courteau

...a few TIPS & TRICKS

Always read through the whole recipe before you start making it. This will give you an idea of what steps lie ahead, what procedures you're going to have to carry out, and how long everything will take. This simple step will help you to avoid potential pitfalls and mistakes along the way.

My number-one tip is that you go out and buy a digital scale to weigh ingredients rather than measure them. The investment, less than $40, will be well worth it. When ingredients are measured by volume the margin of error can be as high as 30 percent, which can make a huge difference to a smaller recipe. In this book we have provided both weights and measurements to try to accommodate everyone, but by sticking to the weights you will achieve better end results and become a better and more consistent baker. We have found that some home scales aren't sensitive enough for very small amounts, so we've stuck to volume measurements for teaspoons and tablespoons, leaving less room for error. In more finicky recipes we have provided conversions for these as well.

Unless the recipe says otherwise, your butter and eggs should always be at room temperature when you start a recipe. If you're in a hurry and your butter is cold, you can warm it up by putting it in a stand mixer bowl and torching the sides of the bowl slightly while mixing with the paddle attachment. Eggs can be placed in a bowl of warm water for a few minutes.

Because everyone's oven is a bit different, actual oven time can fall up to ten minutes on either side of the recommended baking time, so treat it as a guideline only: if a recipe tells you to bake something for 30 minutes, don't automatically take it out at 30 minutes and assume that it's perfectly baked, and if your oven tends to run hot, set your timer to check on it at 25 minutes. Using visual cues or touching to check for doneness should be the determining factor in when your baking is ready.

Most desserts, especially ones made of chocolate, are best eaten at room temperature as this is what allows the aromas and flavours to be released quickly once they hit your taste buds. Obviously, no one wants to eat warm banana cream pie, but leaving a cold dessert out for even 15 minutes before serving it will make a huge difference in flavour.

Sometimes filling a piping bag can feel like a juggling act. Trying to manoeuvre the bag, a spatula, and a bowl with only two hands can result in frustration and a messy piping bag. Solve this problem by using a tall glass or a cutlery holder to hold your bag for you while you fill it.

If you feel like it's hard to pipe on loose parchment paper, use a small amount of a recipe component such as chocolate, batter, or pan spray to 'glue' it to your baking sheet.

a note on EQUIPMENT

The tools I list below are the ones that I deem to be the essentials for any home baker's kitchen. Some of them are a bit of an investment, so if you don't have them all already, try to make things work with what you already have while you build up your collection over time.

Be wary of filling up your kitchen with newfangled gadgets marketed specifically to home bakers—such as egg separators, butter measuring sticks, and battery-operated sifters—that purport to improve upon a classic method that is tried and true. Professional bakers and pastry chefs don't use these types of items for good reason: not only are they often expensive, they can actually make your tasks more complicated, not to mention work poorly and give you inaccurate results.

BAKING SHEETS AND PANS · I like to keep it simple and stick to plain anodized aluminum bakeware lined with parchment paper. It's by far the best for conducting heat and baking things evenly. Silpat or silicone baking mats and moulds also work well. There are many different types of pans out there and they all bake a bit differently, so always keep an eye on your baking times.

CULINARY TORCH · I have two culinary torches in my kitchen: a mini one I use to caramelize sugar and a larger one for torching meringue and heating the side of the mixing bowl when creaming cold butter. You can get most jobs done with the mini torch but the larger one can help speed things up.

DIGITAL SCALE · It's much more accurate to measure by weight than by volume. That's why I recommend using a digital scale over measuring cups. There are plenty of small, affordable digital scales on the market able to handle 1-gram increments. If you have a non-digital scale, that's fine too, but the accuracy will not be as good, something which matters when working with small quantities.

INSTANT-READ DIGITAL THERMOMETER · This is vital when making any recipe calling for specific sugar or chocolate temperatures. These temperatures can fluctuate quickly and with a regular thermometer, by the time you get a reading, it's quite possible that your sugar or chocolate will have gone way above or below the temperature called for. Even if you have an old-style candy thermometer that clips onto the side of a saucepan, you may have a hard time getting an accurate reading if the recipe size is too small. Good instant-read digital thermometers are reasonably priced and will ensure the success of your confections.

HEATPROOF SPATULA · It's useful to have at least one rubber-type heatproof spatula in your kitchen for getting in the corners of pots, stirring hot liquids, and scraping bowls. We use these exclusively at Duchess.

OFFSET SPATULA · Sometimes referred to as an offset palette knife, this simple tool is invaluable in all kinds of situations. Use it to spread creams and fillings evenly, push batter into the corners of pans, lift brownies out of pans, and transfer cakes to a serving plate. They usually come in 4-inch and 8-inch sizes and both are useful to have on hand.

OVEN · All the recipes in this book have been tested using a conventional oven. If you have a convection oven you may need to adjust your baking times and temperatures accordingly.

PASTRY BRUSH · Try to use a pastry brush made with natural bristles. They're gentle on your pastry, hold liquid well, and coat evenly. Silicone pastry brushes don't hold liquid very well, making it difficult to evenly coat your pastry. This can damage the delicately proofed brioches or croissants you worked so hard to make. Natural bristles are a bit trickier to clean than silicone ones, but a good soak in hot water will usually do the trick.

PIPING BAGS · These days, disposable piping bags made of clear plastic are the way to go. They're much more sanitary than the reusable ones and really easy to use. Cake decorators tend to use piping bags that require a coupler so they can easily switch between different piping tips for detailed work, but in the pastry kitchen, these aren't necessary. Simply snip off the end of a piping bag and firmly insert a piping tip. And sometimes even a piping tip isn't necessary: just a hole will do the trick. Try to find 18-inch piping bags (the larger ones) as these are easiest to work with and eliminate the risk of your filling coming out the top.

PIPING TIPS · Having three different piping tips on hand will allow you to decorate and finish most of the recipes in this book: a medium plain round tip (#803 or #804), a large round tip (#809), and a star tip (#826, #827, #828, or #829). In addition, we call for tip #234 for the Mont-Blanc and tip #880 for the St. Honoré.

PLASTIC BOWL SCRAPER · One of these will set you back only a few dollars, but it will come in handy for so many tasks in the kitchen. We use them most for the macaronage process when making macarons, but they're also great for cutting dough, cleaning flour off your counter, and scraping out bowls.

STAND MIXER · It's possible to make many of the recipes in this book using a hand-held mixer, but when it comes to tougher jobs such as mixing bread dough and whipping for long periods of time, you really will need a stand mixer equipped with paddle, whisk, and dough hook attachments.

a note on INGREDIENTS

The quality of the ingredients you use in your baking will directly affect the taste. At Duchess we use only natural ingredients with no preservatives, with the single exception of powdered food colouring (as explained below). The information in this section is designed to help you understand some of the key ingredients used in this book and assist you with your buying choices.

ALMOND FLOUR (FINELY GROUND ALMONDS) Almond flour is the foundation of so many of the products that we make at Duchess. Buying the finest, freshest grind of almond flour you can find is a must. If the grind isn't fine, simply run it through a coffee grinder. At Duchess, we import our own almond flour from California to ensure the freshness and quality.

BUTTER · Unless otherwise noted, use the best quality butter you can find with the highest fat content (*see page 57 for a more detailed discussion on butter*).

CHOCOLATE: In my opinion, the finest baking chocolate in the world is made by Valrhona in France. Over the years we've developed a strong relationship with them and I've been fortunate enough to visit their chocolate factory and pastry school in the Rhône valley. They make a number of different kinds of chocolate, each with its own flavour profile, and in all instances the quality is unbeatable. Their chocolate comes in little callets (one-inch oval disks) that are wonderful for melting and tempering. When we need chips, we often use Callebaut, which we also consider to be of a very high quality (*see page 259 for a discussion on working with chocolate*).

COCOA POWDER: We use alkalized (Dutch-processed) cocoa powder from Valrhona. In our opinion, its colour, high fat content, and deep flavour are unparalleled by any other brand.

COMPOUNDS: Like an extract, a compound is a highly concentrated flavouring, but unlike an extract, it generally doesn't contain alcohol, which gives it a more natural taste and means that it's easier to adjust in a recipe. Compounds are great for flavouring buttercreams, mousses, cake batters, and ganache. At Duchess, we love using fruit-based compounds because they really do taste like cooked-down reduced fruit and have really intense flavour. Compounds can be difficult for home bakers to find. They're often made of synthetic ingredients such as propylene glycol, so make sure you read the ingredients before investing in a few flavours. All-natural compounds can be purchased through our Provisions website or in our shop.

EGG ALBUMEN: Also known as egg white powder, we use this in our macaron recipe to make it more stable. It's not to be confused with the meringue powder commonly sold in cake-decorating stores.

FLOUR: Although we use organic flour for all of our baking at Duchess, we decided that for this book the recipes would be tested with conventional all-purpose flour and bread flour readily available in any grocery store. That's because it can be difficult to come by organic flour and it can vary greatly in consistency from brand to brand.

FOOD COLOURING: When it comes to the ideal of sticking with natural products, food colouring is a tricky one. While we do use natural plant-based liquid colours in some of our baking to brighten things up a little, we have to make an exception for the colouring we use in our macarons. That's because macaron batter is very sensitive to the addition of any liquid extra to the recipe. Instead, we use powdered colours, which are not natural, to achieve the pretty pastel colours—but only in the tiniest amounts. Remember that the more colour you add to a recipe, the more you'll be able to taste it, so try to minimize your use of food colouring.

FRUIT PURÉES: Most fruit purées used by pastry professionals are commercial ones of an extremely high quality and 100 percent natural. We use these exclusively at Duchess.

GELATIN: Powdered and sheet gelatin are both commonly used in the pastry world. Powdered gelatin is easy to find in regular grocery stores and straightforward to use. Sheet gelatin, on the other hand, is usually only found in specialty shops, and because it comes in different strengths, it's potentially confusing for the casual baker. In this book, we keep things easy and call for powdered gelatin only.

LAVENDER: Culinary-grade lavender is easy to find at specialty grocery stores and organic markets. Make sure that the lavender is a bright and vibrant colour when you buy it. It's becoming more common to bring lavender in from overseas that has been sitting on a shelf for months. This lavender will have lost a lot of its brightness and won't provide your baking with the aromatics of fresher lavender.

MARZIPAN: Marzipan can be rolled out and used to cover cakes, similar to fondant. We recommend a marzipan with a minimum of 50 percent almond content. Marzipan may look like almond paste on a store shelf, but they're not the same. Almond paste can't be rolled out and is more commonly used by creaming it with butter or adding it to a batter.

SPICES: Use the freshest spices possible. If your spices are old and stale you may have to drastically increase the quantity that's called for in a recipe to get enough flavour. The best way to check the freshness of your spices is to smell and taste them. Fresh spices have an overwhelmingly strong aroma and intense flavour.

VANILLA: Use only real vanilla extract and the freshest vanilla beans possible for maximum flavour. Vanilla paste, my personal preference, features the addition of vanilla bean seeds for an added flavour boost. In a recipe vanilla paste can be used interchangeably with vanilla extract and 1 Tbsp can replace one whole vanilla bean.

YEAST: In this book we use only fresh yeast, which is inexpensive, easy to use, and contains no additives. Dry yeast, while easy to find, can be confusing to buy and use because there are so many kinds: dry, active dry, instant, rapid-rise... It may also contain additives. You can find fresh yeast in specialty grocery stores, but if you ask at the bakery counter at your local grocery store, they will often sell you a piece from behind the counter. Fresh yeast keeps in the refrigerator for up to two weeks. It can also be frozen, in which case you must increase the recipe quantity by 5 percent as it will lose a bit of its strength. If you wish to use dry yeast instead of fresh, halve the amount and dissolve it in warm liquid to activate it. For example, if the recipe calls for milk, warm it gently in the microwave (not above 46°C/115°F), mix in your dry yeast, and set it aside for five to ten minutes before using in your recipe.

MACAR_oNS

MACARONS · People often ask me, 'If you could eat only one dessert for the rest of your life, what would it be?' I never hesitate— the answer is always 'macarons'. In North America, the macaron is often confused with the macaroon, the American coconut haystack cookie. The French macaron is completely different. It's a small, delicate almond meringue cookie filled with butter- cream, caramel, ganache, or jam. Although macarons have a long history in France, it's only in recent years that they have begun to gain popularity in North America. They are far and away the most loved item on our menu. ◆

all about MACARON SHELLS

MY LOVE AFFAIR WITH MACARONS started when I was living in Tokyo. In Japan, French pastry is held in the highest regard and many of the famous French pastry chefs have a retail location there. My two favourite pastry shops in Tokyo, Ladurée and Pierre Hermé, are satellite shops of the world's two most eminent purveyors of macarons. Their macarons differ quite a lot in texture and character, but I love them equally. Ladurée's shells are light and delicate with subtle fillings while Pierre Hermé's are a bit firmer and contain a much more intense filling.

I spent several months scouring the internet and books for any information I could find on how to make good macarons. My first several attempts were devastating, but with repeated tries, things slowly started to take shape. After four years and over 200 attempts in my home kitchen using a toaster oven, I was able to come up with a recipe that I am proud of.

The two most common methods for making macarons differ in that they are based on either Italian meringue or French meringue. In the Italian meringue method, cooked sugar is poured over egg whites while they're being whipped to make a very stiff and stable meringue. This is a great approach for making very large batches and is the one most commonly used by pastry chefs. In the French meringue method, sugar and egg whites at room temperature are beaten together to form a drier meringue that results in shells with a delicate texture. Although this is the easiest method, it's not suitable for making large batches as it's more finicky.

After experimenting extensively with both methods, the recipe that I settled on is based on the French meringue method. For me, the body, flavour, and texture of the shell just couldn't be beat. We now routinely make up to 1,500 macarons a day at Duchess, and because French meringue tends to be more unstable, we make them by hand in 15 to 20 smaller batches.

TIPS & TRICKS · There's no doubt that the macaron can be a tricky recipe to master for the home baker, so here are a few simple tricks to help avert mishaps.

- Macarons don't like water or humidity. If it's a rainy day or quite humid in your kitchen you may have a difficult time getting the shells to turn out properly.

- The purpose of the food colouring when making the shells is to visually evoke the flavourings added to the fillings. You can also do this by sprinkling crushed nuts, cocoa nibs, or coconut onto the top of the shells after piping.

- Use food coloring sparingly and in powdered form if possible. At Duchess, the only product we offer that contains non-natural food colouring is the macaron—and that's because we can't get natural food colouring in powdered form. If you do use liquid food colouring, use it sparingly as it can change the texture and taste of the shells.

- Make sure your egg whites are at room temperature.

- The meringue must be very stiffly whipped. Under-whipped meringue will result in flat shells with no 'feet' (the word used to describe the slightly ruffled bottom edge of a macaron).

- The macaronage (mixing of the batter) must be done properly. Under- or overmixing the batter is the most common mistake made by beginners. If you undermix your batter, your shells will not have a smooth top and may have a 'spike' that does not disappear during baking. If you overmix the batter it will be too runny and your macarons will be flat and have no feet. During mixing, stop and check to see how your batter 'flows.' It should behave like slow-moving lava and disappear into itself after about 10 seconds.

- Weighing the ingredients will make the recipe more precise and leave less room for error.

french meringue MACARONS

INGREDIENTS

116 g (1¼ cups)	almond flour (finely ground almonds)
180 g (1½ cups)	icing sugar
88 g (about 3 large)	egg whites, at room temperature
35 g (3 Tbsp)	granulated sugar
6 g (1¾ tsp)	egg white powder (egg albumen)
⅛ tsp	powder colour (optional)
	filling of your choice (*see page 30*)

EQUIPMENT · You will need a stand mixer fitted with a whisk attachment, a plastic bowl scraper, two baking sheets, and a piping bag fitted with a medium round piping tip (#803 or #804).

PROCEDURE · You will need a macaron template to help you ensure that your shell sizes are uniform. Cut a piece of parchment paper the size of your baking sheet and trace 20 × 1-inch circles onto it spaced about 1½ inches apart. Place the template on one of the baking sheets and cover it with a second piece of parchment. The shapes will show through for you to use as a guide when piping. You can save this template and reuse it next time you make macarons.

1. Sift the almond flour and icing sugar together into a bowl. If necessary, press the last of the mixture through the sifter with your hands. Discard any larger pieces that won't go through. Set aside.

2. Place the egg whites in a stand mixer bowl. Sift the granulated sugar, egg white powder, and powder colour onto the egg whites.

3. Whip on high until a stiff meringue forms (4 to 4½ minutes). Make sure to whip until it's really stiff (*Photo A*).

4. Pour the sifted almond flour mixture over the meringue and, using a spatula, gently incorporate until just combined (*Photo B*). Transfer the batter to a shallow wide bowl (*Photo C*).

5. Now proceed to the macaronage. With a plastic bowl scraper, smear the batter along the sides of the bowl and scrape it back into the centre. Repeat until the batter becomes shiny and reaches the consistency of slow-flowing lava (*Photos D–I*). How many times you need to do this is highly variable; it might be only a couple of passes or up to a half dozen. If the batter is moving faster than slow-flowing lava, it's been overmixed.

If making a macaron gâteau: Stop mixing your batter a bit early so that it ends up a bit stiffer and able to retain its decorative piping during baking.

6. Immediately proceed to piping the batter. Place the piping bag fitted with the piping tip inside a tall glass and fold the edges of the bag over the rim. Fill the bag with the batter (*Photo J*).

7. Hold the piping bag vertically with the tip ½ inch above the lined baking sheet. With even pressure, while holding your piping bag steady, pipe onto the parchment following the template that you have placed underneath (*Photo K*). At this stage you can sprinkle on additions such as finely chopped nuts, cocoa nibs, or coconut depending on the type of macaron you're making. Go easy on these as the oils can affect the shells.

8. Carefully remove the template from underneath the parchment (*Photo L*), put it on the second baking sheet, cover with another piece of parchment, and repeat step 7. If you have extra batter, feel free to pipe extra shells in empty spaces on the template.

CONTINUED •

9. Bang the baking sheets gently to eliminate any air bubbles from the batter (*Photo M*). Let the shells rest at room temperature until a skin forms on the surface (*Photo N*). This should take 20 to 25 minutes. Test for readiness by touching the top of a shell with your finger. The batter shouldn't feel sticky. While the shells are resting, preheat your oven to 350°F (180°C), positioning the oven rack in the middle of the oven.

10. For baking, use only the middle rack of the oven, baking one sheet at a time. Bake the shells for 8 minutes. Briefly open the oven door to let out steam, rotate the baking sheet, and bake for another 4 minutes. Note: Oven times may vary. If the shells start to brown around the edges, immediately remove them from the oven.

11. Let the shells cool for 20 minutes before carefully peeling them off the parchment paper. At this stage, you can wrap the shells and store them in the freezer for up to a week before filling. Let thaw at room temperature for 20 minutes before assembling.

12. To prepare the macarons for filling, find pairs by matching their sizes. Line the pairs up on a tray. Take one of each pair, flip it over, and gently make an indent in the centre using your thumb (*Photo O*).

13. Fill each indented macaron with the filling you have chosen and cover with its twin, sandwich-style (*Photos P–Q*).

14. If you want to fill your macarons with two different fillings (for example, vanilla buttercream and strawberry jam), simply pipe a ring around the outside of the macaron with one of the fillings and insert the other filling in the middle (*Photo R*).

STORAGE · Filled macarons can be refrigerated for up to three days or frozen for up to a week.

all about
MACARON FILLINGS

THERE ARE SEVERAL DIFFERENT types of filling commonly used in macarons: caramel, jam, a simple ganache, and buttercream. Ganache and buttercream lend themselves well to added flavours. For the home baker, a basic white chocolate ganache is an easy option, and it's what I used for most of my experimenting when I was first learning to make macarons. At Duchess we use a buttercream-based filling. Recipes for white chocolate ganache and buttercream are included in this chapter for you to choose from.

There are a myriad of different ways you can change the flavour of your filling. At Duchess we always have six classic flavours on offer—salted caramel, lemon, rose, pistachio, dark chocolate, and coconut—and three featured flavours each month where we can get creative and come up with some unique tastes. Over the years we've featured over 75 different flavours. Some of our favourites are vanilla bean, passionfruit, pear ginger, black sesame raspberry, and maple. By far our most popular flavour is salted caramel (*pictured left; recipe for salted caramel on page 273*).

All the flavours that we add to our fillings are natural and of the highest quality. Extracts and compounds (*see 'Compounds,' page 18*) are the easiest way to add flavour to a ganache or buttercream, but you can also use jam, reductions, alcohol, freeze-dried fruit, fresh herbs, or even fresh fruit to achieve specific flavours. It's fine to add a bit of liquid to the recipe, but be careful not to add too much as it might affect the overall texture of the filling. Don't hesitate to add more flavouring to your filling if you want it to pack more of a punch.

EASY
white·chocolate
GANACHE

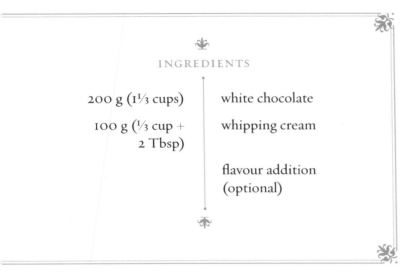

INGREDIENTS

200 g (1⅓ cups)	white chocolate
100 g (⅓ cup + 2 Tbsp)	whipping cream
	flavour addition (optional)

INGREDIENT NOTE · For the white chocolate we use Valrhona 35% Ivoire callets.

PROCEDURE · It's best to make the ganache before starting the macaron shells so that it has the time to set in the refrigerator.

1. Slowly melt the white chocolate over a double boiler or in a microwave on half power. While the chocolate is melting, heat the cream in a saucepan until just scalding.

2. Pour the hot cream over the chocolate in three parts, using a heatproof spatula to mix well between each addition. Mix in any flavour additions at this point. Refrigerate until set.

3. Remove the ganache from the refrigerator about 20 minutes before you're ready to fill the shells so that it can come to room temperature.

STORAGE · Ganache will keep in the refrigerator for up to one week.

FLAVOURING METHODS · Here are some ideas for flavouring your ganache.

— *Extract or Compound* · After the cream has been mixed in, stir in 1 tsp extract or 1 Tbsp compound of your choice. Taste to adjust flavouring.

— *Jam* · After the cream has been mixed in, add 1 to 2 Tbsp jam of your choice.

— *Infusion* · When you heat the cream, add a vanilla bean, loose tea, herbs, or spices. Remove from heat, cover, and let steep for 5 minutes. Strain and immediately add to the melted chocolate.

Buttercream

INGREDIENTS

2	large egg whites
83 g (⅓ cup + 1 Tbsp)	sugar
pinch	salt
226 g (1 cup)	unsalted butter, cubed, at room temperature

FILLS 1 BATCH OF MACARON SHELLS
OR 1 MACARON GÂTEAU

EQUIPMENT · You will need a stand mixer with the whisk and paddle attachments.

PROCEDURE · Before you start the buttercream, make sure the butter is soft and at room temperature.

1. Heat the egg whites, sugar, and salt in a stand mixer bowl fitted over a double boiler, whisking often, until the mixture reaches 55°C (130°F).

2. Remove from heat and fit the bowl to your stand mixer. Using the whisk attachment, whip on high speed until the meringue is shiny and forms stiff peaks.

3. Turn the mixer off and change to the paddle attachment. With the mixer on medium speed, add the butter cubes, a few at a time. Mix until light and fluffy.

STORAGE · Buttercream will keep in the refrigerator for up to one week or in the freezer for up to one month. Bring it to room temperature and whip it up again in the mixer before using it to fill macarons.

BUTTERCREAM FLAVOURS · Here are some ideas for flavouring your buttercream. Simply fold one of the following flavourings into your finished buttercream. If your buttercream was in the refrigerator or freezer, let it come to room temperature and whip it up again in the mixer before folding in the additions.

— *Pistachio* · 1 tsp pistachio extract, 2 Tbsp finely crushed pistachios.

— *Dark Chocolate* · 250 g (1¾ cup) melted dark chocolate (we use Valrhona 66% Caraïbe callets).

— *Almond* · ½ tsp almond extract and 25 g (¼ cup) crushed toasted almonds.

— *Coconut* · 1 tsp coconut extract or 1 Tbsp coconut compound.

— *Vanilla Bean* · Seeds from 1 vanilla bean.

— *Strawberry* · 1 Tbsp wild strawberry compound. When filling the macarons, pipe a ring of buttercream around the outside edge and fill the centre with strawberry jam.

— *Raspberry Lime* · 2 tsp fresh lime zest. When filling the macarons, pipe a ring of buttercream around the outside edge and place half a fresh raspberry in the centre.

— *Earl Grey* · 1 tsp bergamot extract and 1 Tbsp finely ground Earl Grey tea.

MAPLE-BRÛLÉE *marshmallow* MACARONS

MAKES 12 LARGE MACARONS

My cousin and best friend Sarah came up with the idea for these in the early days of Duchess. I was skeptical that we would be able to caramelize the top of a macaron, but lo and behold, it turned out wonderfully—and we had a great new twist on the classic macaron. The use of marshmallow filling and a slightly bigger macaron shell make these fun for everyone to eat. As with all macarons, you can flavour these almost any way you want. I've included a few variations at the end of the recipe for you to try. If you don't have a culinary torch, it's fine to skip the caramelizing.

EQUIPMENT · You will need a stand mixer fitted with a whisk attachment, an instant-read digital thermometer, two piping bags fitted with a medium piping tip (#803 or #804), two baking sheets, and a culinary torch.

TO MAKE THE MACARON SHELLS · You will need a macaron template to help you ensure that your shell sizes are uniform. Cut a piece of parchment paper the size of your baking sheet and trace 12 × 1½-inch circles onto it spaced about 1½ inches apart. Place the template on the baking sheet and cover it with a second piece of parchment. The shapes will show through for you to use as a guide when piping. You can save this template and reuse it next time you make these macarons.

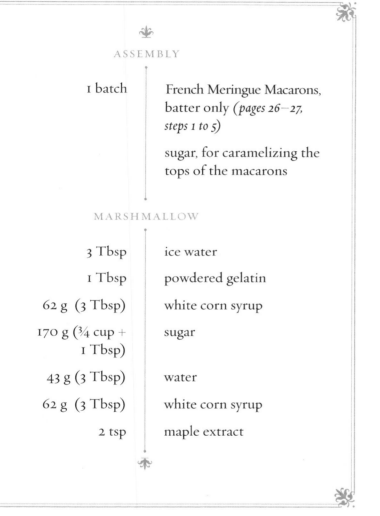

ASSEMBLY

1 batch	French Meringue Macarons, batter only (*pages 26–27, steps 1 to 5*)
	sugar, for caramelizing the tops of the macarons

MARSHMALLOW

3 Tbsp	ice water
1 Tbsp	powdered gelatin
62 g (3 Tbsp)	white corn syrup
170 g (¾ cup + 1 Tbsp)	sugar
43 g (3 Tbsp)	water
62 g (3 Tbsp)	white corn syrup
2 tsp	maple extract

CONTINUED ·

1. As soon as the batter is made and the macaronage has been done, place the piping bag fitted with the piping tip inside a tall glass and fold the edges of the bag over the rim. Fill the bag with the macaron batter.

2. Hold the piping bag vertically with the tip ½ inch above the lined baking sheet. Pipe shells onto the parchment following the template that you have placed underneath.

3. Carefully remove the template from underneath the parchment, put it on the second baking sheet, cover with another piece of parchment, and repeat step 2.

4. Bang the baking sheet gently to eliminate any air bubbles from the batter. Let the shells rest at room temperature until a skin forms on the surface. This should take 20 to 25 minutes. Test for readiness by touching the top of a shell with your finger. The batter should not feel sticky. While the shells are resting, preheat your oven to 350°F (180°C), positioning the oven rack in the middle of the oven.

5. For baking, use only the middle rack of the oven, and bake one sheet at a time. Bake the shells for 9 minutes. Briefly open the oven door to let out steam, rotate the baking sheet, and bake for another 5 minutes. Note: Oven times may vary. If the shells start to brown around the edges, immediately remove them from the oven.

6. Let the shells cool for 20 minutes before carefully peeling them off the parchment paper. At this stage, you can wrap the shells and freeze them for up to a week before filling. Let thaw at room temperature for 20 minutes before assembling.

7. To prepare the macarons for filling, find pairs by matching their sizes. Line the pairs up on a tray. Take one of each pair, flip it over, and gently make an indent in the centre using your thumb. Set aside until the marshmallow is ready.

TO PREPARE THE MARSHMALLOW

8. Make sure the water is ice cold. Put the water in a small microwavable bowl, sprinkle the gelatin over, and stir to dissolve. Set aside at room temperature until firmly set.

9. In a stand mixer fitted with a whisk attachment, place the first measure of corn syrup. Heat the gelatin in a microwave until melted, about 30 seconds, then add it to the corn syrup.

10. In a small saucepan, place the sugar, water, and second measure of corn syrup. Heat the mixture until it reaches a final temperature of between 112° and 115°C (235° and 240°F).

11. Turn the mixer on at low speed and gradually pour the cooked sugar down the side of the mixing bowl. Once all the sugar has been incorporated, turn the speed up to medium-high and mix for 5 minutes, or until the marshmallow looks stiff, light, and fluffy and is pulling away from the sides of the bowl. If you underwhip the marshmallow it will turn out dense rather than airy and soft.

12. Add the maple extract and mix on high speed for 1 minute. You are now ready to pipe the marshmallow. Work quickly as the marshmallow will progressively stiffen and become difficult to pipe.

TO ASSEMBLE THE MACARONS

13. Fill a piping bag with the marshmallow. Fill each indented macaron with marshmallow (*Photo A*) and cover with its twin, sandwich-style.

14. Sprinkle the tops of the macarons with a generous amount of sugar (*Photo B*). Using a culinary torch, toast each macaron until the sugar has caramelized (*Photo C*). This will happen very quickly, so watch carefully to avoid burning or setting alight the tops of the macarons. Hold the torch at a distance until you get comfortable with the flame.

STORAGE · These marshmallow macarons can be kept at room temperature for up to three days. Do not refrigerate as the cooked sugar in marshmallows will melt in a cold and humid environment.

VARIATIONS · Here are some ideas for flavouring your marshmallow macarons. These variations are not intended to be caramelized on top (*omit step 14*).

— *Vanilla Strawberry* · Make pink macaron shells and replace the maple extract with vanilla extract. Pipe the marshmallow in a ring on the outside edge of the bottom shell and pipe strawberry jam into the centre.

— *Coconut Chocolate* · Make white macaron shells sprinkled with coconut and replace the maple extract with coconut extract or compound. Pipe the marshmallow in a ring on the outside edge of the bottom shell and pipe chocolate ganache (*see 'Dark Chocolate Ganache,' page 235*) in the centre.

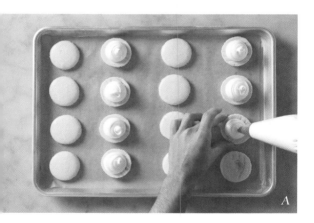

LES MACARON GÂTEAUX · Among our favourite 'cakes' to make at Duchess are our macaron gâteaux. These gâteaux feature two large macaron shells, a top and a bottom, enclosing a set of complementary fillings— a format with endless possibilities. Each season we give our staff the chance to unleash their creativity and come up with a new flavour. In this chapter we've included some of our favourites, all of which can all be made in either a 7-inch or a 4-inch version. ◆

L'AMOUR
macaron gâteau

INGREDIENTS

1 batch	French Meringue Macarons, batter only, coloured pink (*pages 26–27, steps 1 to 5*)
1 batch	Vanilla Bean Buttercream (*page 33*)
1 pint (2 cups)	fresh raspberries
½ batch	Easy White Chocolate Ganache + 1 tsp rose water (*page 31*)
¼ cup	homemade or good-quality raspberry jam
⅓ cup	drained and chopped canned lychees
a few	fresh raspberries, for garnish
2	Chocolate Cigarettes, for garnish (*page 263; optional*)

My biggest inspiration in the pastry world is the famed French pastry chef Pierre Hermé and his ingenious flavour combinations. One of the highlights of my career was getting to spend three days at the Valrhona pastry school in France learning how to make his classic desserts. We were lucky enough to have Pierre Hermé spend a day in the pastry lab sharing with us his passion for pastry and many behind-the-scenes details about his company.

One of my favourite Pierre Hermé creations is the Ispahan, a macaron gâteau filled with lychees, rose ganache, and fresh raspberries. After one taste of that gorgeous flavour combination I just knew we had to try it at Duchess! We used the basic idea and flavours for the Ispahan as a starting point and put our own twist on it to create l'Amour. We make it in a heart shape for Valentine's Day and use our homemade raspberry jam to really boost the flavours. If Pierre Hermé ever got to try our version of his famous dessert, I hope we would do him proud.

EQUIPMENT · You will need a baking sheet and four piping bags, two fitted with medium round piping tips (#803 or #804).

TO MAKE THE MACARON SHELLS · You will need a template for piping the batter. Cut a piece of parchment paper the size of your baking sheet and trace 2 heart shapes onto it, each 7 by 7 inches. Place the template on the baking sheet and cover it with a second piece of parchment. The shapes will show through for you to use as a guide when piping. You can save this template and reuse it next time you make this gâteau.

1. As soon as the batter is made and the macaronage has been done, place a piping bag fitted with a tip inside a tall glass and fold the edges of the bag over the rim. Fill the bag with the macaron batter.

2. Hold the piping bag vertically with the tip ½ inch above the baking sheet. Pipe concentric hearts onto the lined baking sheet following the template that you have placed underneath, starting on the outside and working your way in (*Photo A*).

3. Let the shells rest at room temperature until a skin forms on the surface. This should take 20 to 25 minutes. Test for readiness by touching the top of a shell with your finger. The batter should not feel sticky. While the shells are resting, preheat your oven to 350°F (180°C), positioning the oven rack in the middle of the oven.

4. Bake the shells for 12 minutes. Briefly open the oven door to let out steam, rotate the baking sheet, and bake for another 8 minutes. Note: Oven times may vary. If the shells start to brown around the edges, immediately remove them from the oven.

5. Let the shells cool for 20 minutes before carefully peeling them off the parchment paper. At this stage, you can wrap the shells and freeze them for up to a week before filling. Let thaw at room temperature for 20 minutes before assembling.

TO ASSEMBLE THE GÂTEAU

6. Fill one of the tipless piping bags with rose ganache and the other with raspberry jam. Cut a hole at the end of each bag, making sure the hole for the rose ganache bag is small enough to fit into the centre of a raspberry. Fill a piping bag fitted with a tip with vanilla buttercream.

7. Pipe rose ganache into the centre of each raspberry and arrange the raspberries, filled side down, in a heart shape along the outer edge of the bottom macaron shell (*Photo B*). Add a 'V' shape of filled raspberries inside the heart (*Photo C*).

8. Pipe a thin layer of vanilla buttercream between the rows of raspberries. Top with a thin layer of raspberry jam (*Photo C*).

9. Spoon chopped lychees onto the raspberry jam and top with another thin layer of buttercream (*Photo D*). The filling should now come up even with the tops of the raspberries.

10. Place the second macaron shell on top and press gently, taking care not to crack it.

11. Pipe a small dot of rose ganache on top of the shell and garnish with a fresh raspberry and chocolate cigarettes.

STORAGE · This gâteau will keep for up to three days in the refrigerator.

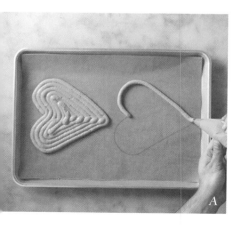

MONT-BLANC
macaron gâteau

The mont-blanc, featuring chestnut purée and whipped cream or meringue, is a very popular dessert in France during the holiday season. Named after Mont Blanc, the highest mountain in the Alps, it stands out in any pastry case with its chestnut spaghetti piping made to resemble a snow-capped mountain. We took this classic dessert and turned it into our holiday macaron gâteau with an added layer of almond cream and dark chocolate.

EQUIPMENT · You will need a baking sheet, five piping bags, and three piping tips: a medium round tip (#803 or #804), a large round tip (#809), and a medium grass tip (#234).

INGREDIENT NOTES · For chestnut purée, look in specialty food stores or at Italian markets. For the dark chocolate we use Valrhona 66% Caraïbe callets.

TO MAKE THE MACARON SHELLS · You will need a template for piping the batter. Cut a piece of parchment paper the size of your baking sheet and trace 2 circles on it, each 7 inches in diameter. Within one of the circles, trace another small circle about 2½ inches from the edge. Place the template on a baking sheet and cover it with a second piece of parchment. The shapes will show through for you to use as a guide when piping. You can save this template and reuse it next time you make this gâteau.

1. As soon as the batter is made and the macaronage has been done, fit a piping bag with a medium round tip (#803 or #804). Place it inside a tall glass and fold the edges of the bag over the rim. Fill the bag with the macaron batter.

2. Hold the piping bag vertically with the tip ½ inch above the baking sheet. Pipe circles in tight spirals onto the lined baking sheet following the template that you have placed underneath, starting on the inside and working your way out. Pipe one of the circles from the centre all the way to the outer edge; for the other, leave the centre unpiped by starting the piping on the inside circle, as per your template *(Photo A, page 47)*.

CONTINUED

INGREDIENTS

1 batch	French Meringue Macarons, batter only *(pages 26–27, steps 1 to 5)*

CHESTNUT CREAM

125 g (½ cup)	chestnut purée
15 g (1 Tbsp)	whole milk
58 g (¼ cup)	whipping cream
2 Tbsp	sugar
2 tsp	cognac
½ tsp	vanilla extract or paste

CHOCOLATE GANACHE

70 g (½ cup)	dark chocolate
77 g (⅓ cup)	whipping cream
20 g (1 Tbsp)	glucose or white corn syrup

155 g (⅔ cup)	whipping cream
1 Tbsp	icing sugar
½ tsp	vanilla extract or paste

ASSEMBLY

1 batch	Almond Buttercream (*page 33*)
	Salted Chocolate Bark, for garnish (*page 262; optional*)

3. Let the shells rest at room temperature until a skin forms on the surface. This should take 20 to 25 minutes. Test for readiness by touching the top of a shell with your finger. The batter should not feel sticky. While the shells are resting, preheat your oven to 350°F (180°C), positioning the oven rack in the middle of the oven.

4. Bake the shells for 12 minutes. Briefly open the oven door to let out steam, rotate the baking sheet, and bake for another 8 minutes. Note: Oven times may vary. If the shells start to brown around the edges, immediately remove them from the oven.

5. Let the shells cool for 20 minutes before carefully peeling them off the parchment paper. At this stage, you can wrap the shells and freeze them in the freezer for up to a week before filling. Let thaw at room temperature for 20 minutes before assembling.

TO MAKE THE CHESTNUT CREAM

6. Combine the chestnut purée, milk, cream, and sugar in a saucepan. On medium-low heat, bring to a boil. Reduce the heat and simmer for 10 to 12 minutes, stirring occasionally, until the mixture is thick and coats the back of a spoon.

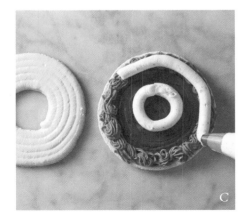

7. Remove from heat and stir in the cognac and vanilla.

8. Cover the chestnut cream and refrigerate for 2 to 3 hours, until set.

TO MAKE THE CHOCOLATE GANACHE

9. Slowly melt the chocolate over a double boiler or on half power in a microwave. In a saucepan, heat the whipping cream and glucose until just scalding.

10. Pour the hot cream over the melted chocolate in three parts, mixing with a spatula between additions until smooth. Refrigerate for 2 hours, or until set.

TO ASSEMBLE THE GÂTEAU

11. Place the whipping cream, icing sugar, and vanilla in a stand mixer bowl fitted with a whisk attachment. Whip on medium-low speed until soft peaks form.

12. Fit a piping bag with the large plain round tip (#809) and fill with almond cream. Fit another bag with the grass tip (#234) and fill with chestnut cream. Fill one of the untipped piping bags with chocolate ganache and the other with whipped cream and cut a small hole at the end of each.

13. Pipe a thin layer of chocolate ganache over the bottom of the macaron shell, leaving about ½ inch of room around the edge (Photo A). Pipe a thick layer of chestnut cream in a ring around the outside of the shell (Photo B).

14. Pipe a thick layer of almond buttercream in a ring on top of the chestnut cream. Add a second, smaller ring on the inside, leaving a gap between the two rings (Photo C).

15. Pipe whipped cream to fill the gaps (Photo D). Place the second macaron shell on top and press gently, taking care not to crack it.

16. Pipe a heaping mound of whipping cream in the centre and enclose with piped chestnut cream (Photos E–F). Garnish with chocolate bark.

STORAGE · This gâteau will keep in the refrigerator for up to three days.

st. lucia

MACARON
GÂTEAU

INGREDIENTS

1 batch	French Meringue Macarons, batter only, coloured yellow (*pages 26–27, steps 1 to 5*)
1 batch	Salted Chocolate Bark, for garnish (*page 262; optional*)

MANGOES

2 medium *or* 1 large	ripe mangoes, peeled and diced
1 tsp	vanilla extract or paste
1 Tbsp	rum (optional)

YOGURT LIME BUTTERCREAM

1 batch	Buttercream (*page 32*)
100 g (⅓ cup + 1 Tbsp)	Greek yogurt
	zest of 2 limes

EQUIPMENT · You will need a baking sheet and two piping bags fitted with medium round piping tips (#803 or #804).

TO MAKE THE MACARON SHELLS · You will need a template for piping the batter. Cut a piece of parchment paper the size of your baking sheet and trace 2 circles onto it, each 7 inches in diameter. Within one of the circles, trace another small circle about 2½ inches from the edge. Place the template on the baking sheet and cover it with a second piece of parchment. The shapes will show through for you to use as a guide when piping. You can save this template and reuse it next time you make this gâteau.

1. As soon as the batter is made and the macaronage has been done, place a piping bag fitted with a tip inside a tall glass and fold the edges of the bag over the rim. Fill the bag with the macaron batter.

2. Hold the piping bag vertically with the tip ½ inch above the baking sheet. Pipe circles in tight spirals onto the lined baking sheet following the template that you have placed underneath, starting on the inside and working your way out. Pipe one of the circles from the centre all the way to the outer edge; for the other, leave the centre unpiped by starting the piping on the inside circle, as per your template (*Photo A*).

3. Let the shells rest at room temperature until a skin forms on the surface. This should take 20 to 25 minutes. Test for readiness by touching the top of a shell with your finger. The batter should not feel sticky. While the shells are resting, preheat your oven to 350°F (180°C), positioning the oven rack in the middle of the oven.

4. Bake the shells for 12 minutes. Briefly open the oven door to let out steam, rotate the baking sheet, and bake for another 8 minutes. Note: Oven times may vary. If the shells start to brown around the edges, immediately remove them from the oven.

5. Let the shells cool for 20 minutes before carefully peeling them off the parchment. At this stage, you can wrap the shells and freeze them for up to a week before filling. Let thaw at room temperature for 20 minutes before assembling.

TO ASSEMBLE THE GÂTEAU

6. Toss the diced mangoes with the vanilla and the rum. Set aside.

7. Fold the lime zest and the Greek yogurt into the buttercream.

8. Fill a piping bag with with the yogurt lime buttercream. Pipe a thin layer of buttercream to cover the inside of the shell. Pipe buttercream dots 1 inch wide and 1 inch high in a ring on the outer edge of the bottom shell, leaving about ½ inch of room between each dot (*Photo B*).

9. Spoon diced mangoes around the edge between the buttercream dots and spread a layer into the middle of the gâteau (*Photo C*), reserving about ¼ cup.

10. Place the second macaron shell on top and press gently, taking care not to crack it.

11. Pipe additional buttercream into the centre of the shell, spoon additional diced mangoes on top (*Photo D*), and decorate with salted chocolate bark.

STORAGE · This gâteau will keep in the refrigerator for up to three days.

Printemps
MACARON GÂTEAUX

MAKES 4 × 3-INCH GÂTEAUX

INGREDIENTS

1 batch	French Meringue Macarons, batter only, coloured green (*pages 26–27, steps 1 to 5*)
	crushed pistachios

SPICED STRAWBERRIES

300 g (1 cup)	finely diced strawberries (or a fruit of your choice)
1 Tbsp	honey
pinch	ground cloves

ASSEMBLY

½ batch	Cream Cheese Frosting (*page 113*)
½ batch	Pistachio Buttercream (*page 33*)
	White Chocolate Petals, for garnish (*page 264; optional*)

This macaron gâteau is inspired by the strawberries and pistachios that are featured in one of my favourite French desserts, the fraisier. When we make this gâteau, with its green colour and fresh strawberries, it's a sure sign that spring is around the corner!

EQUIPMENT · You will need a baking sheet, two piping bags fitted with medium round tips (#803 or #804), and one piping bag fitted with a star tip (any of #826 to #829).

TO MAKE THE MACARON SHELLS · You will need a template for piping the batter. Cut a piece of parchment paper the size of your baking sheet and trace 8 × 3-inch circles onto it. Place the template on the baking sheet and cover it with a second piece of parchment. The shapes will show through for you to use as a guide when piping. You can save this template and reuse it next time you make this gâteau.

1. As soon as the batter is made and the macaronage has been done, place a piping bag fitted with a tip inside a tall glass and fold the edges of the bag over the rim. Fill the bag with the macaron batter.

2. Hold the piping bag vertically with the tip ½ inch above the baking sheet. Pipe circles in tight spirals onto the lined baking sheet following the template that you have placed underneath, starting in the centre and working your way out. Pipe four circles from the centre all the way to the outer edge; for the other four, start piping just a little out from the centre to leave a ½-inch hole in the middle (*Photo A*).

3. Lightly sprinkle the shells with crushed pistachios.

CONTINUED

4. Let the shells rest at room temperature until a skin forms on the surface. This should take 20 to 25 minutes. Test for readiness by touching the top of a shell with your finger. The batter should not feel sticky. While the shells are resting, preheat your oven to 350°F (180°C), positioning the oven rack in the middle of the oven.

5. Bake the shells for 9 minutes. Briefly open the oven door to let out steam, rotate the baking sheet, and bake for another 5 minutes. Note: Oven times may vary. If the shells start to brown around the edges, immediately remove them from the oven.

6. Let the shells cool for 20 minutes before carefully peeling them off the parchment paper. At this stage, you can wrap the shells and freeze them for up to a week before filling. Let thaw at room temperature for 20 minutes before assembling.

TO ASSEMBLE THE GÂTEAUX

7. Combine the diced strawberries with the honey and ground cloves. Set aside for 15 minutes to allow the flavours to develop.

8. Take the second piping bag with a medium round tip and fill with the pistachio buttercream. Fit a piping bag with the star tip and fill with the cream cheese frosting.

9. Alternating between the pistachio buttercream and the cream cheese frosting, pipe dots 1 inch wide and 1 inch high in a ring on the outer edge of the bottom shell (*Photo B*).

10. Pipe a thin layer of cream cheese frosting to cover the middle of the inside of the shell.

11. Spoon the diced strawberries into the middle until they come up even with the tops of the piped dots (*Photo C*), reserving a few tablespoons for garnish.

12. Place the second macaron shell on top and press gently, taking care not to crack it.

13. Spoon reserved strawberries into the centre of the shell (*Photo D*). Pipe dots of pistachio buttercream on the top and garnish with a white chocolate petal.

STORAGE · These gâteaux will keep in the refrigerator for up to three days.

CROISSANTS

THE FLAKY, DELICATE, BUTTERY CROISSANT is the epitome of French pastry. When we visit Paris, our first stop is always at our favourite little boulangerie to indulge in an authentic croissant. For me, the perfect croissant has what seems like a thousand flaky layers, a light, almost ethereal quality, a rich buttery taste, and lots of flavour.

Croissant dough is laminated, a process by which layers of dough and butter are alternated to make pastry. Although typically dough for danishes has the added richness of eggs, at Duchess we make our danishes out of the same laminated dough that we use for our croissants —we just shape the dough differently. We really like the flavour of our croissant dough and use it as a versatile base for all of our croissant and danish recipes. ◆

LAMINATED DOUGHS

LAMINATED DOUGHS · Learning to make croissant dough requires quite a bit of practice. There are so many variables that will affect the outcome, such as how hot your kitchen is, the temperature of the liquids you're using, and the kind of butter you're using. You also need to get comfortable with the technique of laminating dough. Puff pastry is the easiest kind of laminated dough to make because it doesn't contain yeast. If you have never made a laminated dough, it might be a good idea to start with puff pastry (see pages 244–247), and then move on to croissant dough once you get the hang of it. Here are a few simple tips for working with laminated doughs:

— Weigh your ingredients rather than measuring them out by volume. It's important to be as accurate as possible when working with yeasted doughs.

— Use butter with the highest butterfat content you can find (between 82% and 84%).

— Use fresh yeast, not dry (see 'Yeast,' page 19).

— The most important step in making croissant dough is the laminating process. The more you practice, the more you'll get a feel for the dough and what the temperature of your butter needs to be.

— When you're first starting out, don't worry too much about the sizes and shapes of your croissants and danishes. Instead try to focus on mastering the laminating process—the shaping will come with practice.

— This recipe is quite small, yielding only seven or eight croissants or danishes. It's best to stick with this quantity until you've got a good grasp of the butter temperature and the laminating technique. Once you've got your footing, you can start doubling or even tripling the recipe.

A NOTE ON BUTTER · After spending four years in Japan and having access to amazing butter from France and Spain, coming back to Canada and trying to find the same quality of butter was really frustrating. In Canada, the law is that all butter must contain a minimum of 80% butterfat. In reality, there are only a few producers that exceed this in any significant way, and depending on where you live, it can be really tricky to get your hands on their butter. Increasing the butterfat level to 82% or 84% may not sound like much, but when it comes to croissant dough and puff pastry it makes all the difference in the world.

We make our croissants primarily with commercial butter from New Zealand that contains 84% butterfat. That butter isn't available to the home baker in Canada. We can, however, recommend Stirling Creamery's European-Style 84% unsalted butter or Cow's Creamery's 84% unsalted butter, both of which are available in a few smaller specialty grocery stores, including our own Provisions shop. If you can find one of these butters, your end result will be far superior.

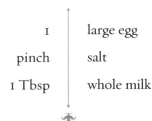

BUTTER PLAQUE

165 g (¾ cup)	unsalted butter, cold

DOUGH

18 g (1 Tbsp + 1 tsp)	fresh yeast
74 g (¼ cup + 1 Tbsp)	warm water
53 g (⅓ cup)	bread flour, sifted
30 g (2 Tbsp)	unsalted butter, at room temperature
21 g (1 Tbsp + 2 tsp)	sugar
6 g (1¼ tsp)	salt
94 g (¼ cup + 2 Tbsp)	whole milk, at room temperature
240 g (1½ cups)	all-purpose flour, sifted

EGG WASH

1	large egg
pinch	salt
1 Tbsp	whole milk

CROISSANTS

MAKES ENOUGH DOUGH FOR 7–8
CROISSANTS OR DANISHES

Making croissants requires advance planning as there are a number of steps to execute—though with plenty of waiting time in between for you to go off and do something else. For this recipe, most of the dough preparation is done the day before baking. Leaving the shaped dough in the refrigerator overnight will allow the flavours to develop and you can wake up the next morning and bake fresh croissants or danishes.

EQUIPMENT · You will need a stand mixer fitted with a dough hook attachment, an instant-read digital thermometer, a resealable plastic bag 7 inches in width, and a baking sheet.

INGREDIENT NOTE · If possible use butter with 82%–84% butterfat *(see 'A Note on Butter,' page 57)*.

TO PREPARE THE DOUGH · Remove the butter for the butter plaque from the refrigerator and set aside.

1. To make the starter, crumble the yeast into a large bowl. Add the warm water and mix until dissolved.

2. Add the sifted bread flour and mix with a wooden spoon or spatula. The dough will look slightly lumpy, a bit like pancake batter. Cover and let rise for 45 minutes, or until doubled in volume.

3. While the starter is rising, weigh out the butter, sugar, and salt together in a bowl. Using a spatula, mix until well combined. If you add the sugar and salt directly to the starter, you run the risk of killing the yeast in the dough: the butter prevents this by creating a fat buffer.

4. Once the starter has doubled in size, transfer it to a stand mixer bowl.

5. Add the milk to the starter along with the butter mixture and the sifted all-purpose flour. Mix on low speed until the dough comes together, stopping the mixer at least once to scrape down the sides of the bowl. After all the dry ingredients have been incorporated, continue to mix on low for 5 more minutes.

6. Remove the dough from the mixer and shape it into a round ball. Transfer the dough to a lightly oiled bowl, cover, and let rise for 1 to 1½ hours, until doubled in size.

7. While the dough is rising, prepare your butter plaque. Put the set-aside butter into a resealable plastic bag 7 inches wide (*Photo 1*). With the bag's zip open to allow air to escape, use a rolling pin to press the butter into the bottom corners of the bag. Once the butter is well into the corners, continue to roll it until it's 5 inches in length from the bottom of the bag. Use a bench scraper to create a perfect edge at the 5-inch mark (*Photos 2–3*). Seal the bag and refrigerate.

8. Once the dough has doubled in size, lightly flour a work surface and roll the dough into a rectangular shape about 7½ by 10½ inches—that is, just over double the size of your butter plaque. Line a baking sheet with parchment paper. Transfer the dough to the baking sheet and cover well with plastic wrap. Place in the freezer for 25 to 30 minutes, and then transfer to the refrigerator for an additional 30 minutes. When you transfer the dough to the refrigerator, take out the butter plaque and proceed immediately to step 9.

CONTINUED ·——————

9. Cut the bag open along the sides, remove the bag's top layer, and set the butter plaque on the counter to sit at room temperature, keeping it on the bottom half of the bag (*Photos 4–6*). The amount of time the butter plaque needs to sit depends on how warm your kitchen is. Getting this right is key to the success of your croissant dough. The idea is to get your butter to the right temperature so that it's pliable enough to roll into the dough without cracking, but not so warm that it leaks out of the sides during rolling. The dough also needs to remain cold enough so that it doesn't proof during the lamination process. Every five minutes, check the butter plaque's texture by pressing into it lightly with your finger. It's ready when it feels like modeling clay and an indent forms with little pressure (*Photo 6*). Immediately proceed to the next step when your butter reaches this point.

10. Remove the dough from the refrigerator, unwrap it, transfer it to a lightly floured surface, and press out any air. Make sure it measures 7½ by 10½ inches and adjust if necessary.

11. Flip the butter plaque onto one side of the dough and gently peel away the plastic bag (*Photo A*). Cut the dough in half (*Photo B*) and flip the cut half over onto the butter plaque, like a sandwich (*Photo C*).

12. Firmly crimp the edges of the dough to hold in the butter plaque and keep the dough together. Using a rolling pin, gently press the top of the dough to start joining the dough and the butter together (*Photo D*). Flip the dough over and repeat on the other side. At this point you should be able to feel whether your butter is pliable enough to move with the dough. If it feels too hard, let it rest at room temperature for another 5 minutes.

13. Roll the dough out to an 8-by-20-inch rectangle (*Photo E*). Trim off about ½ inch of dough from the short edges (*Photo F*).

14. Fold the short edges over to meet in the middle of the rectangle (*Photo G*). Using the middle seam, close the two sides like a book. This is called a book fold (*Photos H—I*). Wrap the dough, place it on a baking sheet, and return it to the refrigerator for 20 minutes.

15. Remove the dough from the refrigerator. Again, roll the dough into an 8-by-20-inch rectangle, making sure you are rolling in the direction of the seam edge (*Photo J*). Trim the short edges again, and fold the dough in thirds like you're folding a letter. This is called a single fold (*Photos K–L*). Wrap the dough, place it on a baking sheet, and return it to the refrigerator for 30 to 40 minutes.

CONTINUED

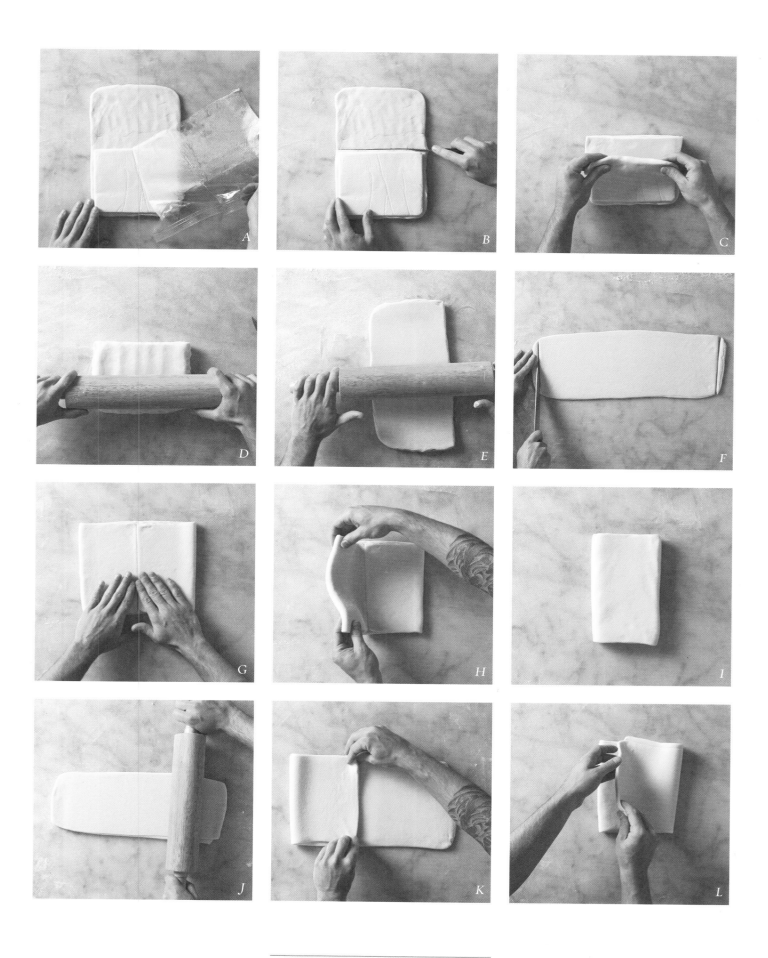

16. On a lightly floured surface, roll the dough into a rectangle measuring about 9 by 18 inches, making sure you are rolling in the direction of the seam edge. If at any point the dough becomes either difficult to roll or too warm, wrap in plastic, place on a tray, and rest in the refrigerator for 10 to 15 minutes. This will allow the gluten to relax while ensuring that the butter remains cold, preserving the lamination.

17. Cut the dough into 7 or 8 even triangles according to your preference *(Photo L)*.

18. In the middle of the base of each triangle cut a small slit about ½ inch long *(Photo M)*. Pick up a dough triangle and stretch it out by pulling gently *(Photo N)*.

19. Gently pull the corners of the slit away from each other *(Photo O)*. Starting at the base of the triangle, roll the dough all the way up to the tip *(Photos P–Q)*. Place the shaped croissants on the lined baking sheet with the tips underneath, spacing them out evenly *(Photo R)*.

20. Cover the shaped croissants with plastic wrap and refrigerate overnight. Alternatively, freeze them for a maximum of two weeks before baking, transferring them to the refrigerator and leaving them there overnight before proofing.

21. The next day, fill a pan with the hottest water you can get out of your tap (not boiling) and place it on the bottom surface of your oven. Remove the croissants from the refrigerator, unwrap them, put the baking sheet on an oven rack, and close the oven door.

22. Let the croissants proof in the oven for 1½ to 2 hours, until they are doubled in size, the layers are starting to separate on the sides of the croissants, and a slight depression forms to the touch *(Photo S)*. Try not to open the oven door for the first 45 minutes as you want the steam to create a humid environment inside the oven.

23. Once proofed, remove the bowl of water and the croissants from the oven. Preheat your oven to 425°F (220°C).

24. In a small bowl, whisk the egg, salt, and milk to make egg wash. Using a pastry brush, gently brush the wash over the tops of the croissants *(Photo T)*.

25. Position the baking sheet on your oven's middle rack. Bake for 16 minutes, rotate the baking sheet, and bake for another 3 to 4 minutes, until the croissants are a deep golden brown. Serve warm out of the oven plain or with your favourite jam.

STORAGE · Croissants are best eaten the day they are made. They can be stored at room temperature for up to three days and re-warmed slightly in the oven before serving.

PAINS *au* CHOCOLAT

INGREDIENT NOTES · For the dark chocolate callets we use Valrhona 64% Manjari, and for the milk chocolate callets we use Valrhona 40% Jivara.

TO ROLL AND SHAPE THE DOUGH · Line a baking sheet with parchment paper.

1. On a lightly floured surface, roll out the croissant dough to a 6½-by-24-inch rectangle, making sure you are rolling in the direction of the seam edge. If at any point the dough becomes either difficult to roll or too warm, wrap in plastic, place on a tray, and rest in the refrigerator for 10 to 15 minutes. This will allow the gluten to relax while ensuring that the butter remains cold, preserving the lamination.

2. Cut the dough into 8 even rectangles (*Photo A*).

3. Lay three callets or a chocolate stick along the bottom of the shorter edge of each rectangle. Fold the dough over, roll up each pain au chocolat (*Photo B*), and arrange them evenly on the lined baking sheet with the ends tucked underneath.

4. Cover the shaped pains au chocolat and refrigerate overnight. Alternatively, freeze them for a maximum of two weeks before baking, transferring them to the refrigerator and leaving them there overnight before proofing.

5. To finish, follow the instructions on how to proof and bake croissants (*page 62, steps 21 to 25*).

INGREDIENTS

1 batch	Croissant Dough (*pages 58–61, up to step 15*)
24	dark or milk chocolate callets *or*
8	chocolate croissant sticks

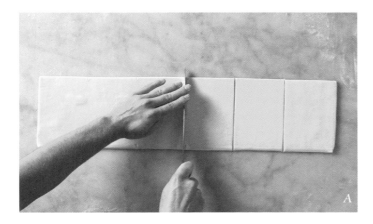

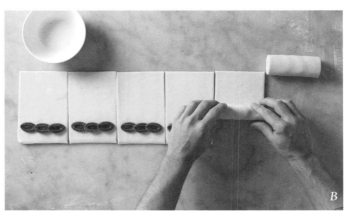

CROISSANT · BREAD · PUDDING

MAKES 8 SERVINGS

This bread pudding is by far my biggest temptation when working at Duchess. It doesn't have that eggy texture and sogginess so common to bread pudding. Instead, we've created one that is rich, sweet, and buttery. It's all the more indulgent because we use day-old croissants rather than plain bread.

EQUIPMENT · You will need a 9-by-9-inch baking dish. Alternatively, use strong standalone paper baking cups to make individual bread puddings as we do at Duchess.

PROCEDURE · Preheat the oven to 350°F (180°C). Butter the baking dish.

1. In a large bowl, whisk together the sugar and eggs. Add the milk, vanilla, brandy, and pecans and mix until well combined.

2. Add the croissant chunks and chocolate and toss using your hands to make sure that all the pieces of croissant are well coated. Let soak for 15 minutes.

3. Pour the mixture into the baking dish and bake for 45 minutes, or until the top is golden brown and crispy.

STORAGE · This bread pudding will keep at room temperature for up to three days.

INGREDIENTS

250 g (1¼ cups)	sugar
3	large eggs
242 g (1 cup)	whole milk
2 tsp	vanilla extract or paste
2 tsp	brandy
128 g (1 cup)	roughly chopped pecans
5 or 6 (about 5 cups)	day-old croissants or pains au chocolat, cut into 1-to-2-inch chunks
80 g (½ cup)	milk or dark chocolate chips

ALMOND CROISSANTS

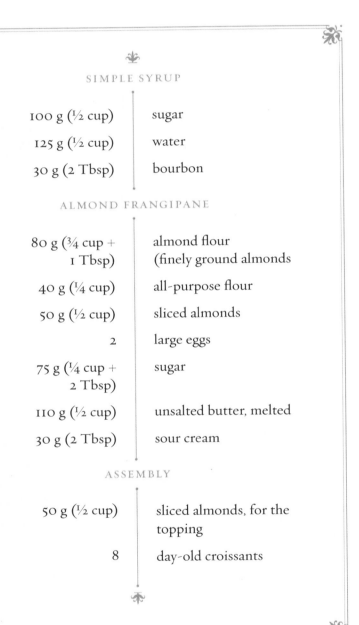

SIMPLE SYRUP

100 g (½ cup)	sugar
125 g (½ cup)	water
30 g (2 Tbsp)	bourbon

ALMOND FRANGIPANE

80 g (¾ cup + 1 Tbsp)	almond flour (finely ground almonds
40 g (¼ cup)	all-purpose flour
50 g (½ cup)	sliced almonds
2	large eggs
75 g (¼ cup + 2 Tbsp)	sugar
110 g (½ cup)	unsalted butter, melted
30 g (2 Tbsp)	sour cream

ASSEMBLY

50 g (½ cup)	sliced almonds, for the topping
8	day-old croissants

These almond croissants always disappear quickly at Duchess. We use day-old croissants, and that second baking gives them that lovely, crispy texture which makes them so appealing. You can omit the bourbon if you wish.

EQUIPMENT · You will need a stand mixer fitted with a whisk attachment and a baking sheet.

PROCEDURE · Preheat your oven to 350°F (180°C). Line the baking sheet with parchment paper.

1. To make simple syrup, place the sugar, water, and bourbon in a small saucepan. Heat until the syrup just comes to a boil. Remove from heat and set aside to cool.

2. In a bowl, mix together the almond flour, all-purpose flour, and the 50 g (½ cup) measure of sliced almonds. Set aside.

3. Put the eggs and sugar in a stand mixer bowl and whip on medium speed until frothy. Slowly stream in the melted butter and mix until well incorporated.

4. Remove the bowl from the mixer and gently fold in the dry ingredients and the sour cream until just combined.

5. Using a serrated knife, slice each croissant in half horizontally so the top and the bottom are nicely even. Brush the insides of the croissant halves generously with the cooled simple syrup. Arrange the bottom halves evenly on the lined baking sheet.

6. Spread a generous layer of the almond frangipane over each bottom half, reserving about ½ cup for finishing. Cover each with a top half and press down firmly to flatten. It's fine if frangipane comes out the sides and looks a little messy—it will all bake into a delicious, crispy pastry.

7. Spread an additional heaping tablespoon of frangipane over the top of each croissant and sprinkle generously with the second 50 g (½ cup) measure of the almonds.

8. Bake for 28 to 30 minutes, until the frangipane is golden brown. Serve warm or at room temperature.

STORAGE · These croissants are best eaten the day they are made. They can be stored at room temperature for up to three days and re-warmed slightly in the oven before serving.

AMARENA CHERRY DANISHES

ASSEMBLY

1 batch	Croissant Dough *(pages 58–61, up to step 15)*
1 × 300 g jar	Amarena cherries

FRANGIPANE

55 g (¼ cup)	unsalted butter
50 g (¼ cup)	sugar
55 g (½ cup + 1 Tbsp)	almond flour (finely ground almonds)
2¼ tsp	cornstarch
1	large egg
½ tsp	vanilla extract or paste
1 tsp	rum

EGG WASH

1	large egg
pinch	salt
1 Tbsp	whole milk

The Amarena is a small, dark-coloured sour cherry from Italy. Look for amarenas in Italian markets and grocery stores, where they come packed in a delicious syrup that is great to pour over ice cream or fruit. They are my favourite type of cherry to use in pastries. We've added almond frangipane to make these danishes all the more irresistible.

EQUIPMENT · You will need a stand mixer fitted with a paddle attachment, two baking sheets, and a piping bag.

TO MAKE THE FRANGIPANE

1. Place the butter and sugar in a stand mixer bowl. Cream on medium speed until light and fluffy, scraping down the sides of the bowl as needed.

2. Add the almond flour and cornstarch and mix until combined.

3. In a separate bowl, whisk together the egg, vanilla, and rum.

4. With the mixer on low speed, slowly add the egg mixture, mixing until well combined. You now have almond frangipane.

5. Refrigerate the frangipane until you're ready to proof your dough.

CONTINUED

TO ROLL AND SHAPE THE DOUGH · Line the baking sheets with parchment paper.

6. On a lightly floured surface, roll out the croissant dough to an 18-by-9-inch rectangle, making sure you are rolling in the direction of the seam edge. If at any point the dough becomes either difficult to roll or too warm, wrap in plastic, place on a tray, and rest in the refrigerator for 10 to 15 minutes. This will allow the gluten to relax while ensuring that the butter remains cold, preserving the lamination.

7. Cut the dough into 8 (4½-inch) squares. Fold each square in half diagonally (Photos A–B).

8. Take a sharp knife and cut slits parallel to the equal edges of each triangle, not quite meeting at the point (Photos C–D).

9. Open the triangle back to a flat square shape (Photo E). Take the thin triangular edge and pull it over the centre to line up with the other side (Photos F–G). Repeat on the other side (Photos H–I). Arrange the danishes on the lined baking sheets as you prepare them, spacing them out evenly.

10. Cover the shaped danishes with plastic wrap and refrigerate overnight. Alternatively, freeze them for a maximum of two weeks before baking, transferring them to the refrigerator and leaving them there overnight before proofing.

TO PROOF AND BAKE THE DANISHES

11. The next day, remove the frangipane from the refrigerator and allow it to come to room temperature while you proof the danishes.

12. Fill a pan with the hottest water you can get out of your tap (not boiling) and place it on the bottom surface of your oven. Remove the danishes from the refrigerator, unwrap them, put the baking sheets on oven racks, and close the oven door.

13. Let the danishes proof in the oven for 1½ to 2 hours, until they are doubled in size, the layers are starting to separate on the sides of the danishes, and a slight depression forms to the touch (Photo J). Try not to open the oven door for the first 45 minutes as you want the steam to create a humid environment inside the oven.

14. Once proofed, remove the danishes and the bowl of water from the oven. Preheat the oven to 425°F (220°C).

15. Fill a piping bag with the frangipane, cut a small hole off the end, and pipe frangipane to fill the centre of each danish, making sure to get in all the corners (Photo K). Gently press 4 Amarena cherries into the frangipane (Photo L).

16. In a small bowl, whisk the egg, salt, and milk to make egg wash. Using a pastry brush, gently brush the wash over the edges of the danishes.

17. Place the baking sheets in the oven staggered on the middle and lower racks. Bake for 16 minutes, rotate the baking sheets, and bake for another 3 to 4 minutes, until the danishes are a deep golden brown. Serve warm out of the oven.

STORAGE · These danishes are best eaten the day they're made. They can be stored at room temperature for up to three days and re-warmed slightly in the oven before serving.

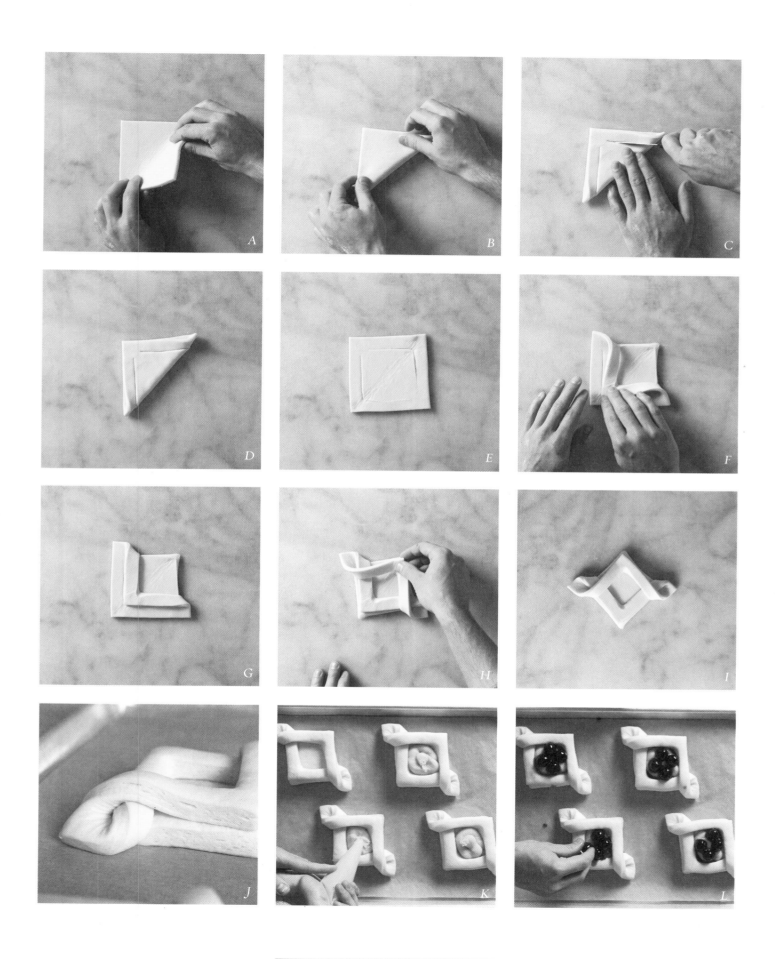

PEAR *cream* *cheese* DANISHES

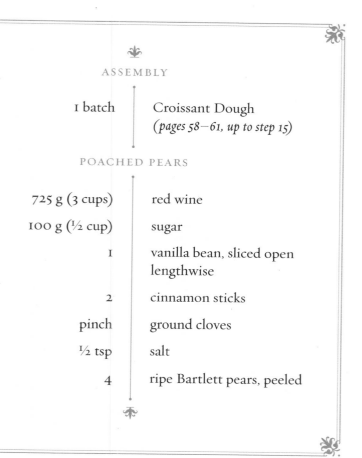

1 batch	Croissant Dough *(pages 58–61, up to step 15)*

POACHED PEARS

725 g (3 cups)	red wine
100 g (½ cup)	sugar
1	vanilla bean, sliced open lengthwise
2	cinnamon sticks
pinch	ground cloves
½ tsp	salt
4	ripe Bartlett pears, peeled

MAKES 8 DANISHES

EQUIPMENT · You will need a stand mixer fitted with a paddle attachment and two baking sheets.

TO POACH THE PEARS · Prepare a *cartouche*—a paper lid to keep the pears submerged in the syrup while they are poaching. Do this by cutting a circle out of parchment paper sized to just fit inside a small saucepan. Cut a small hole in the centre for venting *(see page 197, Photo B)*.

1. In a saucepan only just large enough to fit the pears, combine the wine, sugar, vanilla bean, spices, and salt. Bring to a boil. Reduce the heat to minimum and add the whole pears, one at a time. Fit the *cartouche* snugly overtop.

2. Simmer on low for 1 hour, or until the pears are soft. To keep from overcooking the pears, the simmering temperature must be as low as possible and the syrup must not boil.

3. Remove from heat and let the pears cool in their syrup for a few hours at room temperature or overnight in the refrigerator.

CONTINUED

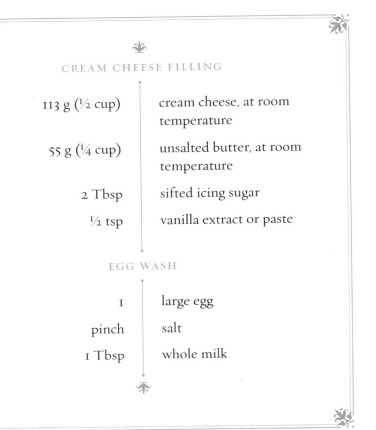

CREAM CHEESE FILLING

113 g (½ cup)	cream cheese, at room temperature
55 g (¼ cup)	unsalted butter, at room temperature
2 Tbsp	sifted icing sugar
½ tsp	vanilla extract or paste

EGG WASH

1	large egg
pinch	salt
1 Tbsp	whole milk

TO MAKE THE CREAM CHEESE FILLING · It's very important that your cream cheese and butter both be at room temperature. If they aren't, you'll end up with lumpy filling.

4. Place the cream cheese and butter in a stand mixer bowl and whip on medium speed for 2 minutes.

5. Turn the mixer off and add half the icing sugar. Mix on low speed until well combined. Repeat with the remaining icing sugar.

6. Add the vanilla, turn the mixer up to medium-high, and whip for another 30 seconds, or until light and fluffy. Scrape down the sides of the bowl as needed.

TO ROLL AND SHAPE THE DOUGH · Line two baking sheets with parchment paper.

7. On a lightly floured surface, roll out the croissant dough to an 18-by-9-inch rectangle, making sure you're rolling in the direction of the seam edge. If at any point the dough becomes either difficult to roll or too warm, wrap in plastic, place on a tray, and rest in the refrigerator for 10 to 15 minutes. This will allow the gluten to relax while ensuring that the butter remains cold, preserving the lamination.

8. Cut the dough into 8 (4½-inch) squares.

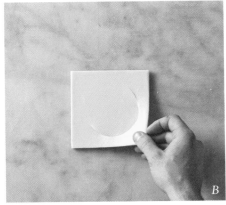

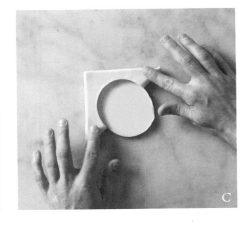

9. Using a ramekin or a small bowl as a guide, cut a half circle out of the centre of each square, lining the ends of the half-circle up diagonally with the corners of the square (*Photo A*).

10. Grab the free corner and fold it in half over the circle, producing a triangle with two layers of dough and a half circle sticking out (*Photos B–C*). Place the danishes on the lined baking sheets as you prepare them, spacing them out evenly.

11. Cover the shaped danishes with plastic wrap and refrigerate overnight. Alternatively, freeze them for a maximum of two weeks before baking, transferring them to the refrigerator and leaving them there overnight before proofing.

TO PROOF AND BAKE THE DANISHES

12. The next day, fill a pan with the hottest water you can get out of your tap (not boiling) and place it on the bottom surface of your oven. Remove the danishes from the refrigerator, unwrap them, put the baking sheets on oven racks, and close the oven door.

13. Let the danishes proof in the oven for 1½ to 2 hours, until they are doubled in size, the layers are starting to separate on the sides of the danishes, and a slight depression forms to the touch. Try not to open the oven door for the first 45 minutes as you want the steam to create a humid environment inside the oven.

14. While the dough is proofing, remove the pears from the poaching liquid and pat dry with a paper towel. Slice each pear in half and remove the core. Starting about 2 cm from the top of the pear, slice into 1 cm sections, leaving the slices attached at the top. Spread the pear slices out like a fan (*Photo D*).

15. Once proofed, remove the danishes and the bowl of water from the oven. Preheat the oven to 425°F (220°C).

16. Scoop a heaping tablespoon of cream cheese filling onto the circle of each danish (*Photo E*). Gently push a fanned pear half onto the cream cheese (*Photo F*).

17. In a small bowl, whisk the egg, salt, and milk to make egg wash. Using a pastry brush, gently brush the wash over the edges of the danishes.

18. Place the baking sheets in the oven staggered on the middle and lower racks. Bake for 16 minutes, rotate the baking sheets, and bake for another 3 to 4 minutes, until the danishes are a deep golden brown. Serve warm out of the oven.

STORAGE · These danishes are best eaten the day they are baked.

Spinach & Feta Danishes

INGREDIENTS

1 batch	Croissant Dough (*pages 58–61, up to step 15*)

SPINACH FILLING

1 Tbsp	unsalted butter
½	garlic clove, finely chopped
¼ tsp	salt
¼ tsp	ground black pepper
1	green onion, finely chopped
1 Tbsp	finely chopped fresh dill
225 g (⅓ cup)	packaged frozen spinach, thawed, drained, and chopped
95 g (¾ cup)	feta cheese

EGG WASH

1	large egg
pinch	salt
1 Tbsp	whole milk

TO PREPARE THE SPINACH FILLING

1. Over medium-low heat, melt the butter in a saucepan. Add the garlic and sauté for about 1 minute, until soft. Add the salt and pepper, remove from heat, and let rest for 5 minutes.

2. Return the saucepan to medium heat and add the green onion and dill. Sauté for 1 minute and remove from heat.

3. Put the spinach in a bowl and pour the butter-herb mixture over top. Crumble in the feta cheese and mix to combine. Adjust the salt and pepper.

TO ROLL AND SHAPE THE DOUGH · Line a baking sheet with parchment paper.

4. On a lightly floured surface, roll out the croissant dough to a 7-by-21-inch rectangle, making sure you are rolling in the direction of the seam edge. If at any point the dough becomes either difficult to roll or too warm, wrap in plastic, place on a tray, and rest in the refrigerator for 10 to 15 minutes. This will allow the gluten to relax while ensuring that the butter remains cold, preserving the lamination.

5. Cut the dough into 12 (3½-inch) squares.

6. Arrange 6 of the squares on the lined baking sheet, spacing them out evenly. Scoop a heaping tablespoon of the spinach filling into the centre of each square (*Photo A*).

7. Cover each portion of filling with one of the remaining squares, angling it to form a star shape (*Photo B*). Cut 3 small vents on top (*Photo C*).

8. Cover the shaped danishes with plastic wrap and refrigerate overnight. Alternatively, freeze them for a maximum of two weeks before baking, transferring them to the refrigerator and leaving them there overnight before proofing.

9. The next day, fill a pan with the hottest water you can get out of your tap (not boiling) and place it on the bottom surface of your oven. Remove the danishes from the refrigerator, unwrap them, put the baking sheet on an oven rack, and close the oven door.

10. Let the danishes proof in the oven for 1½ to 2 hours, until they are doubled in size, the layers are starting to separate on the sides of the danishes, and a slight depression forms to the touch. Try not to open the oven door for the first 45 minutes as you want the steam to create a humid environment inside the oven.

11. Once proofed, remove the bowl of water and the danishes from the oven. Preheat the oven to 425°F (220°C).

12. In a small bowl, whisk the egg, salt, and milk to make egg wash. Using a pastry brush, gently brush the wash over the tops and the bottom corners of the danishes.

13. Position the baking sheet on your oven's middle rack. Bake for 16 minutes, rotate the baking sheet, and bake for another 3 to 4 minutes, until the danishes are a deep golden brown (*Photo D*). Serve warm out of the oven.

STORAGE · These danishes are best eaten the day they are baked.

Brioche & Bread

ALL ABOUT BRIOCHE · Brioche is a rich, buttery, sweet egg dough. It's quite versatile: it can easily be made into a loaf or shaped into boules, buns, or braids, and can be eaten plain or enhanced with all kinds of different fillings. Because of its high sugar and fat content, it is baked at a lower temperature than most other kinds of bread. Nothing beats it warm out of the oven with your favourite jam. Leftover brioches are also tasty reheated in the oven, toasted, or made into French toast. ◆

CLASSIC BRIOCHE

You can make brioches in standard 4-inch brioche moulds (we use tin-plated fluted moulds; silicone moulds also work well), a standard 12-cup muffin pan, or paper baking cups. If you use the paper cups, make sure they are structurally strong enough to stand up on their own. You can also hand-shape the dough to make larger-sized buns.

We like to enhance plain brioche dough with fillings to make some of our more popular breakfast pastries. We've provided some of our favourite filling recipes on the pages to follow. They are flexible, so feel free to use them as inspiration for your own ideas.

EQUIPMENT · You will need a stand mixer fitted with a dough hook and two baking sheets. You will also need 12 × 4-inch brioche moulds or sturdy paper baking cups or a standard 12-cavity muffin pan. Alternatively, you can hand-shape the brioche dough into larger-sized buns.

INGREDIENTS

13 g (1 Tbsp)	fresh yeast, crumbled
30 g (2 Tbsp)	whole milk, warmed
250 g (1½ cups + 1 Tbsp)	all-purpose flour
30 g (2 Tbsp)	sugar
1 tsp	salt
3	large eggs
145 g (⅔ cup)	unsalted butter, cubed, at room temperature
1	large egg yolk
	sugar, for garnish (for plain, unfilled boules)

PROCEDURE

1. In a small bowl, stir the yeast into the warm milk until dissolved.

2. In a stand mixer bowl, mix together the flour, sugar, and salt by hand. Make a well in the centre and add the eggs and dissolved yeast.

3. Fit the bowl on the stand mixer and mix on low speed until all the ingredients are well combined. Stop the mixer at least once to scrape down the sides.

4. Still on low speed, gradually add the butter, a few cubes at a time.

5. Once all the butter has been added, turn the mixer up to medium speed and continue mixing until the dough is smooth and shiny and has pulled away from the sides of the bowl (Photo A). This should take 15 to 20 minutes.

6. Shape the dough into a ball and transfer to a lightly oiled bowl. Cover and let rise at room temperature for 1 hour, or until doubled in size (Photo B).

7. Punch down the dough, cover, and refrigerate for at least 4 hours.

CONTINUED

8. Remove the dough from the refrigerator and transfer it to a lightly floured surface. Punch it down a second time and shape it into a rectangle (*Photo C*). At this point the dough is ready to use, but it can also be wrapped in plastic wrap lightly sprayed with oil and stored in the refrigerator for up to two days or in the freezer for up to one week.

9. Butter and flour the brioche moulds or muffin pan. If you're using paper baking cups, spray them with vegetable oil. Set aside.

10. Using a knife or a bench scraper, divide the dough into 12 portions of about 50 g each.

11. Lightly flour your work surface. Cup your hand over one ball of dough and, keeping your hand in a claw shape, roll the dough in one spot using the pad of your thumb and the sides of your hand (*Photo D*). This motion will shape your dough into a nice ball. The trick is to make sure that you keep your surface floured to the right level: too much and there won't be enough traction to shape the dough; not enough and the dough will stick to the counter and tear.

12. *If making plain or filled brioches in a mould:* Place the rolled balls into the mould seam side down so that the tops of the brioche boules will be smooth. Gently press down into the mould (*Photo E*).

    If making free-form plain or filled brioches: Place the rolled balls seam side down on a parchment-lined baking sheet. Flatten gently with your hand.

13. To proof the boules, fill a pan with the hottest water you can get out of your tap (not boiling) and place it on the bottom surface of your oven. If using moulds, place these on two baking sheets (or only one, if using a muffin pan), position them on oven racks, and close the oven door. Let the boules proof in the oven for about 1½ hours, or until doubled in size. Try not to open the oven door for the first hour as you want the steam to create a humid environment inside the oven.

14. Once proofed, remove the bowl of water and the boules from the oven. Preheat your oven to 385°F (195°C).

15. In a small bowl, whisk the egg yolk. Using a pastry brush, gently brush the yolk over the tops of the boules *(Photo F)*.

    If making plain brioches in a mould: Lightly sprinkle the boules with sugar, being careful to sprinkle only the boules and not the pan (if sugar bakes onto the sides of the brioches, the baked brioches can be difficult to unmould).

    If making filled brioches (free-form or in a mould): Peel the frozen brioche fillings out of their paper liners or pop them out of their silicone moulds. If you have trouble getting the fillings out of the moulds, wait 5 minutes for them to defrost slightly. Firmly press a portion of the filling into the centre of each boule *(Photos G–H; see filling recipes on pages 87 and 89)*.

16. Bake for 15 to 18 minutes, until the brioches are a deep golden brown. Unmould immediately. Brioches are best served warm.

STORAGE · Brioches are best eaten the day they're baked. If it's a day or two old brioche works well toasted or made into French toast or bread pudding.

TIPS & TRICKS · Here are a few simple tips for making the perfect brioches:

— Because the dough is yeasted, try to weigh your ingredients rather than measuring them by volume. You will get more consistent results.

— Use the best quality butter possible. A higher fat content will really improve the texture and flavour of your brioches *(see 'A Note on Butter,' page 57)*.

— Use a good stand mixer with a dough hook attachment. Mixing the dough is very difficult by hand and a hand mixer might not be able to handle the workload.

— Make sure you mix the brioche dough for the full 15 to 20 minutes. It needs to feel soft, smooth, and warm and have good elasticity.

— The fillings need to be frozen when you add them to the proofed brioche dough. Have them already frozen before you start on the dough. This will allow you to focus on the proofing time and not be fiddling with preparing fillings when your dough has finished proofing and is ready to be filled.

Apple Crème Brûlée
BRIOCHE FILLING

We love the classic crème brûlée custard and wanted to incorporate it into a breakfast pastry. Our solution? Pair it with fresh apples and crumb and use it as brioche filling—a sure hit at any brunch.

EQUIPMENT · You will need a mini-muffin pan or silicone mould and a baking sheet.

PROCEDURE · Preheat your oven to 225°F (110°C). If using a mini-muffin pan, line with muffin cups (the ones made out of parchment paper are much easier to peel off the fillings than the standard paper ones). Line the baking sheet with parchment paper.

CRÈME BRÛLÉE CUSTARD

130 g (½ cup + 1 Tbsp)	whipping cream
2	large eggs
65 g (¼ cup + 1 Tbsp)	sugar
2 tsp	brandy or bourbon
1 tsp	vanilla extract or paste
1 cup	peeled, cored and diced Granny Smith apple
1 Tbsp	unsalted butter
pinch	ground cinnamon

CRUMB TOPPING

28 g (¼ cup)	old-fashioned rolled oats
3 Tbsp	all-purpose flour
2 Tbsp	firmly packed golden brown sugar
pinch	ground cinnamon
2 Tbsp	unsalted butter

1. In a bowl, prepare the crème brûlée custard by whisking together the whipping cream, eggs, sugar, brandy, and vanilla.

2. Distribute the custard evenly between the 12 cavities of the mini-muffin pan or mould. Bake for 30 minutes, or until the centre is slightly set. Set aside to cool.

3. While the custard is baking, sauté the diced apple, butter, and cinnamon over medium heat until the apple has softened slightly. Set aside.

4. Preheat your oven to 375°F (180°C). In a bowl, combine the dry ingredients for the crumb topping. Add the butter and, using your hands, work it into the dry ingredients until large clumps form.

5. Spread the crumb on the lined baking sheet and bake for 10 minutes, or until light golden brown.

6. Once the custard has cooled, top each portion, still in its cavity, with a heaping tablespoon of diced apple and a sprinkling of crumb. Freeze for at least 4 hours before using to fill brioche boules (*see page 85, step 15*).

STORAGE · These filling portions can be kept frozen for up to one month.

RASPBERRY CHOCOLATE
brioche filling

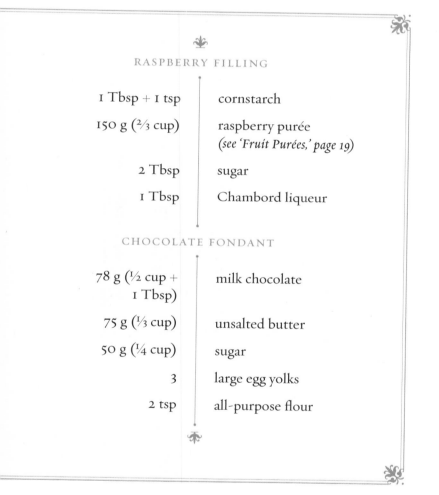

RASPBERRY FILLING

1 Tbsp + 1 tsp	cornstarch
150 g (⅔ cup)	raspberry purée *(see 'Fruit Purées,' page 19)*
2 Tbsp	sugar
1 Tbsp	Chambord liqueur

CHOCOLATE FONDANT

78 g (½ cup + 1 Tbsp)	milk chocolate
75 g (⅓ cup)	unsalted butter
50 g (¼ cup)	sugar
3	large egg yolks
2 tsp	all-purpose flour

EQUIPMENT · You will need a stand mixer with a paddle attachment, two piping bags, and a mini-muffin pan or silicone mould. If using a mini-muffin pan, line with muffin cups (the ones made out of parchment paper are much easier to peel off the fillings than the standard paper ones).

INGREDIENT NOTES · For the milk chocolate we use Valrhona 40% Jivara callets. If you can't find raspberry purée you can make your own by cooking raspberries until soft and straining them through a fine mesh sieve.

PROCEDURE

1. In a small bowl, dissolve the cornstarch in about 1 Tbsp of water. In a saucepan over medium heat, bring the raspberry purée and sugar to a simmer. Whisking constantly, add the dissolved cornstarch, bring to a boil, and boil for 2 minutes. Remove from heat and whisk in the liqueur.

2. Cool slightly. Fill a piping bag with the mixture, cut a small hole at the bottom of the bag, and pipe the mixture evenly into the bottoms of 12 of the cavities of your mini-muffin pan or mould.

3. To make the chocolate fondant, slowly melt the chocolate over a double boiler or in a microwave *(see 'Melting Chocolate,' page 259)*. Set aside.

4. Put the butter and sugar in a stand mixer bowl. Cream on medium speed. Add the egg yolks one at a time, scraping down the sides of the bowl between each addition.

5. Turn the mixer down to low and slowly stream in the melted chocolate. Scrape down the sides of the bowl as needed. Add the flour and mix until just combined.

6. Fill a piping bag with chocolate fondant. Pipe the fondant evenly over the raspberry filling portions. You might have a bit of batter left over. Freeze for at least 4 hours before using to fill brioche boules *(see page 85, step 15)*.

STORAGE · These filling portions can be kept frozen for up to one month.

BRIOCHE PÉPIN

The year before we opened Duchess I was dreaming about what the menu would include, and I knew that this brioche would have to be on it. It's commonly called brioche au chocolat or brioche aux pépites, but somewhere along the way we started referring to the pépites (chocolate chips) as pépins (chocolate seeds), and the name has stuck ever since. Eaten warm out of the oven, these are the ultimate breakfast indulgence.

INGREDIENTS

1 batch	Classic Brioche Dough (*pages 83–84, steps 1 to 8*)
1 batch	Pastry Cream (*pages 188–189, steps 1 to 7*)
140 g (¾ cup)	milk chocolate chips
2	large egg yolks

INGREDIENT NOTE · We use Callebaut milk chocolate chips.

PROCEDURE · Line two jelly roll pans or baking sheets with edges with parchment paper.

1. Lightly flour a work surface and roll out the brioche dough into a 20-by-10-inch rectangle (*Photo A*).

2. Scoop the pastry cream onto the dough and, using an offset spatula, spread it right to the edges (*Photo B*).

3. Sprinkle the chocolate chips evenly over the pastry cream (*Photo C*).

4. In one quick motion, fold the dough in half (*Photo D*). It's fine if a bit of pastry cream spills out the edges.

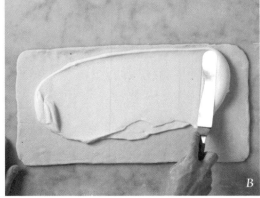

5. Using a sharp knife, slice the dough into pieces about 2½ inches wide *(Photo E)*. Using a long knife or offset spatula, gently transfer the brioche pieces to the lined jelly roll pans, spacing them about 1 inch apart.

6. To proof the brioches, fill a pan with the hottest water you can get out of your tap (not boiling) and place it on the bottom surface of your oven. Place the jelly roll pans on oven racks and close the oven door. Let the brioches proof in the oven for about 1 hour, or until doubled in size. Try not to open the oven door for the first 45 minutes as you want the steam to create a humid environment inside the oven.

7. Once proofed, remove the bowl of water and the brioches from the oven. Preheat your oven to 385°F (195°C).

8. In a small bowl, whisk the egg yolk. Using a pastry brush, generously brush the yolk over the tops of the brioches *(Photo F)*. Bake for 15 to 18 minutes, until the tops are a dark golden brown. Serve slightly warm.

STORAGE · Brioche is best eaten the day it's baked. It will keep at room temperature for up to two days.

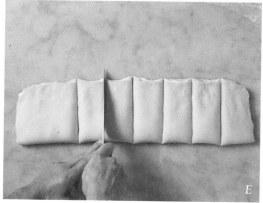

FRENCH
—*loaf*

We often get asked why we don't offer more bread at Duchess. My answer is that our focus is on being a pâtisserie and not a boulangerie. Baking bread is a profound art requiring years of study and dedication as well as different equipment, and we have the deepest respect for the wonderful bread bakers in our city who are true masters of the craft. That is why we have limited our bread offerings to one simple recipe that we shape into French loaves, baguettes, and boules—staples in the French diet.

From start to finish, the recipe takes a day and a half to complete, but don't let that discourage you. The dough is very easy to make and you don't need to spend a lot of time in the kitchen: mostly the dough is just left to rest.

INGREDIENTS

233 g (¾ cup + 3 Tbsp)	hot water (45°C/110°F)
333 g (2½ cups)	bread flour
12 g (1 Tbsp)	fresh yeast, crumbled
1¼ tsp	salt

EQUIPMENT · You will need a stand mixer with a dough hook attachment and a baking sheet.

TO MAKE THE DOUGH

1. Place the hot water and flour in a stand mixer bowl. Mix on low speed until the dough comes together. Cover and set aside for 45 minutes.

2. Put the bowl back on the mixer and add the crumbled yeast. Mix on low speed for about 15 minutes.

3. Add the salt and mix for another 2 minutes.

4. Shape the dough into a ball and transfer to a lightly oiled bowl. Cover and let rise at room temperature for 1 hour, or until doubled in size.

5. Punch the dough down and reshape it into a tight ball. Put it back in the bowl, cover, and refrigerate overnight or for up to 12 hours. The dough will be doubled in size (*Photo A*).

CONTINUED

Line the baking sheet with parchment paper.

6. The next day, punch the dough down and, using a bench scraper, divide it into two portions (*Photo B*). Place the portions on a lightly floured surface, shape each into a tight ball (*Photo C*), cover with a tea towel or plastic wrap, and let rest for 30 minutes.

7. On a lightly floured surface, flip one of the balls over and flatten into a circle (*Photo D*).

8. Fold the sides of the circle into the centre, slightly overlapping, and press down firmly (*Photos E–F*).

9. Fold the top of the dough into the centre and press down with your thumbs (*Photo G*). Fold the dough down a second time, leaving an inch on the bottom, and press down with your thumbs (*Photo H*). For the final fold, roll the dough over so that the seam is down and seal by pressing down with your fingers or the heel of your hand (*Photo I*).

10. Roll the dough out with your fingers into its final shape (*Photo J*). Repeat from step 7 with the second dough ball and place the two loaves on a lined baking sheet (*Photo K*).

11. To proof the loaves, fill a pan with the hottest water that will come out of your tap (not boiling) and place it on the bottom surface of your oven. Position the loaves on an oven rack and close the oven door. Let the dough proof in the oven for 1½ hours, or until doubled in size. Try not to open the oven door for the first hour as you want the steam to create a humid environment inside the oven.

12. Once proofed, remove the loaves from the oven. Preheat your oven to 425°F (220°C).

13. Using a sharp serrated knife or a razor blade, score the middle of each loaf about ¼ inch deep (*Photo L*).

14. Bake the loaves for 25 to 30 minutes, until dark golden brown.

STORAGE · These loaves are best eaten the day they are baked, but they can keep at room temperature for up to three days or in the freezer for up to a month.

VARIATIONS · To make these variations, mix in the listed ingredients by hand after step 3.

— *Olive* · 100 g (¾ cup) chopped pitted olives (we like to use garlic olives).

— *Cheese & Herb* · 100 g (1 cup) gruyère or aged cheddar cheese in ½-inch cubes and 1 tsp each fresh rosemary, parsley, and thyme.

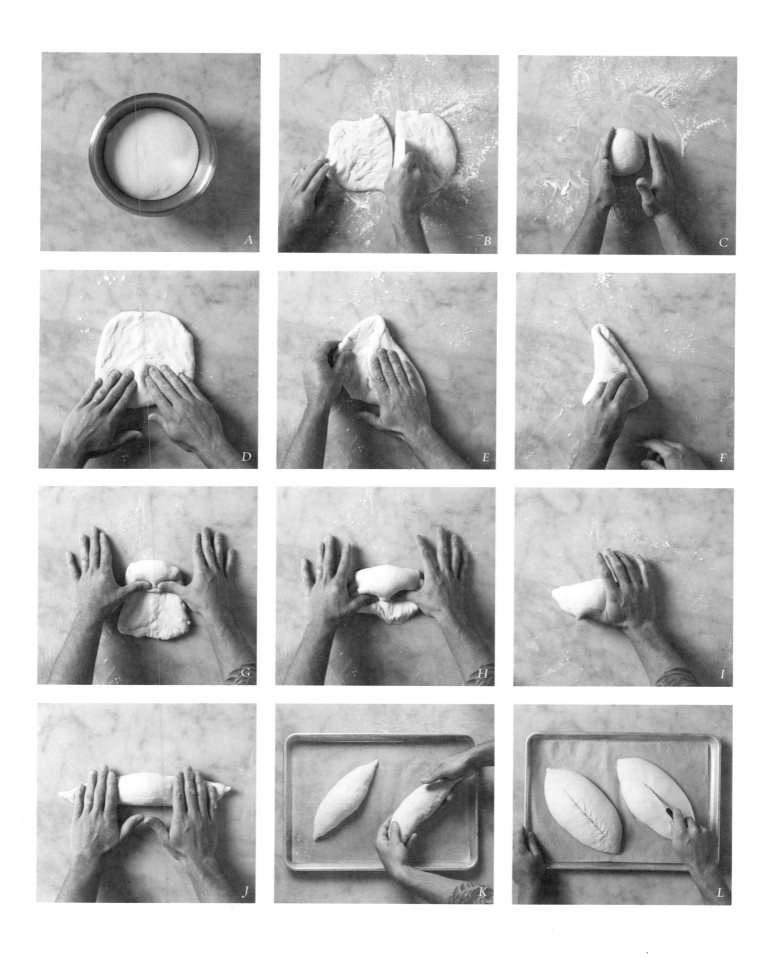

Tartiflette

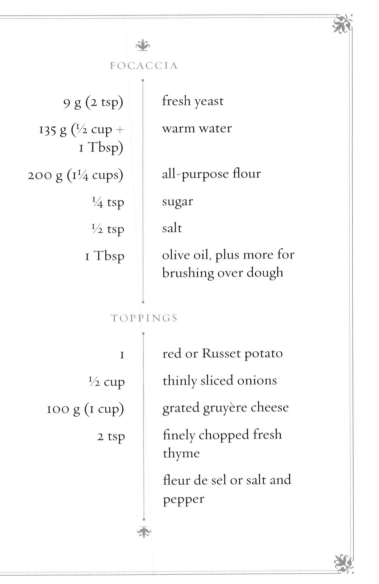

FOCACCIA

9 g (2 tsp)	fresh yeast
135 g (½ cup + 1 Tbsp)	warm water
200 g (1¼ cups)	all-purpose flour
¼ tsp	sugar
½ tsp	salt
1 Tbsp	olive oil, plus more for brushing over dough

TOPPINGS

1	red or Russet potato
½ cup	thinly sliced onions
100 g (1 cup)	grated gruyère cheese
2 tsp	finely chopped fresh thyme
	fleur de sel or salt and pepper

When I visit France in the winter, two of my favourite dishes to eat on a chilly day are tarte flambée and tartiflette. Tarte flambée is a type of flatbread from the Alsace region typically topped with cheese and a white cream sauce, while tartiflette is a creamy layered potato gratin dish from the Alps made with rich, soft reblochon cheese, potatoes, onions, and lardons. We took elements from both these dishes to come up with our own version of tartiflette. We use a thin focaccia base with my favourite toppings, which of course are flexible. This recipe can be easily doubled to make two pans.

We like to slice our onion and potato thinly for this recipe. We find that it's best to use a mandolin for this. If you don't have one, slice them as thinly as you can by hand.

EQUIPMENT · You will need a stand mixer fitted with a dough hook, a baking sheet, and a mandolin slicer (optional).

PROCEDURE · Line the baking sheet with parchment paper.

1. In a stand mixer bowl, stir the yeast into the warm water until dissolved.

2. Add the flour, sugar, salt, and olive oil and mix on medium-low speed. Once the dough has come together, stop the mixer and scrape down the sides. Continue to mix on medium speed for 15 to 20 minutes, until the dough is smooth and elastic.

3. Shape the dough into a ball and transfer to a lightly oiled bowl. Cover and let rise at room temperature for 45 minutes to 1 hour, until doubled in size.

4. Once the dough has doubled in size, transfer it to a lightly floured surface and roll it into an 8-by-14-inch rectangle (Photo A).

5. Place it on the lined baking sheet and, using your fingers, gently make dents in the top of the dough (Photo B). Brush generously with olive oil, and set aside to rise for another 30 minutes (Photo C).

CONTINUED

6. While your dough is rising, slice the potatoes using a mandolin or as thinly as possible by hand. Boil them in salted water for 3 to 5 minutes, until tender. Using a slotted spoon or fine mesh strainer, transfer the potato slices into a bowl of ice water. Once cooled, transfer the slices to a paper towel.

7. Once the dough has risen, preheat your oven to 425°F (220°C).

8. Arrange the sliced potatoes evenly over the dough. Top with the onion and spread the grated cheese evenly over the top. Sprinkle with fresh thyme, fleur de sel, and pepper (*Photos D–F*).

9. Bake the tartiflette for 25 to 30 minutes, until the cheese is golden and bubbling. Cut into 4 pieces. Serve warm.

STORAGE · Tartiflette is best eaten the day it's made. It can be refrigerated for up to two days but will need to be reheated under the broiler before serving.

Tea Time

Hummingbird
— LOAVES

These easy-to-make mini loaves, inspired by the well-known Southern hummingbird cake, are one of our most popular creations. We once tried to take it off our menu, but it almost caused a riot among its many dedicated fans—so we brought it back. The crushed pineapple keeps this loaf really moist and the generous amount of cream cheese frosting makes it feel like an indulgence.

INGREDIENTS

320 g (2 cups)	all-purpose flour
200 g (1 cup)	sugar
¾ tsp	baking soda
¾ tsp	salt
½ tsp	ground cinnamon
65 g (½ cup)	chopped pecans
2	large eggs
112 g (½ cup)	vegetable oil
1 tsp	vanilla extract or paste
125 g (½ cup)	canned crushed pineapple (not drained)
2	medium bananas, mashed

ASSEMBLY

1 batch	Cream Cheese Frosting (*page 113*)
	whole pecans, for garnish

EQUIPMENT · You will need a mini-loaf pan with 6 × 5-by-3-inch cavities. If you don't have one, you can use 2 × 9-by-5-inch loaf pans. To frost the loaves, you may wish to use a piping bag fitted with a star tip (#826–#829).

PROCEDURE · Butter and flour the loaf pan or spray it with vegetable oil. Preheat your oven to 350°F (180°C).

1. In a large bowl, whisk together the flour, sugar, baking soda, salt, cinnamon, and chopped pecans. Set aside.

2. In a separate bowl, combine the eggs, oil, vanilla, pineapple, and banana and mix well.

3. Pour the wet ingredients over the dry and, using a spatula or a spoon, mix until just combined.

4. Using an ice cream scoop or a spoon, fill the mini-loaf cavities halfway up.

5. Bake for 25 to 30 minutes, until golden brown and a toothpick comes out clean (add 10 to 15 minutes if making two large loaves). Let cool completely before unmoulding.

6. Frost or pipe the tops of the loaves with the frosting and top each one with a whole pecan.

STORAGE · These loaves will keep at room temperature for up to three days unfrosted or one day frosted. You can always keep the frosting in the refrigerator and frost the loaves as needed, bringing the frosting to room temperature first.

VANILLA
madeleines

You'll always remember the first time you eat a moist, buttery madeleine warm out of the oven. These tiny French tea cakes make a lovely little snack that won't ruin an appetite. They are also a great finisher after a big meal. The batter is quick and easy to prepare, bakes up in no time flat, and freezes really well. It's also ideal for introducing all kinds of flavours—I've included a few suggested additions at the end of the recipe to get you started.

EQUIPMENT · You will need a 16 or 24-cavity madeleine pan. These are becoming easier to find in specialty kitchen stores and online. It's hard to come up with an alternative pan to use as it's the distinctive shell-like shape that makes the madeleine unique; however, a mini-muffin pan will also work.

PROCEDURE · The batter will need to rest in the refrigerator for at least 3 hours before baking. When ready to bake, preheat your oven to 400°F (205°C). Grease and flour the madeleine pan.

INGREDIENTS

160 g (1 cup)	all-purpose flour
½ tsp	baking powder
4	large eggs, at room temperature
150 g (¾ cup)	sugar
150 g (⅔ cup)	unsalted butter, melted and cooled
2 tsp	vanilla extract or paste
100 g (½ cup)	sugar
120 g (½ cup)	water

1. Mix the flour and baking powder in a small bowl and set aside.

2. Whisk the eggs and first measure of sugar in a bowl until well combined. Add the butter, vanilla, and any flavour additions (*see suggestions on the next page*) and whisk until well combined.

3. Make a well in the centre of the dry ingredients, and whisk in the wet ingredients. Mix until well combined.

4. Cover with plastic wrap and refrigerate for at least 3 hours.

5. While the batter is resting, make simple syrup by placing the second measure of sugar and the water in a small saucepan. Bring to a boil to dissolve the sugar. Remove from heat and set aside to cool.

6. Using a small ice cream scoop or a spoon, fill each madeleine cavity to about three-quarters full. Bake for 10 to 12 minutes, until they are golden around the edges. You'll see a bump rise up in the middle of each madeleine—a sign of success!

7. Once baked, immediately unmould the madeleines by gently tapping the pan on the counter. Dip each one in the simple syrup to coat well. Madeleines are best served warm, but may also be served at room temperature.

STORAGE · Madeleines are best eaten the day they're baked. The batter will keep for up to three days in the refrigerator or up to one month in the freezer.

SUGGESTED FLAVOUR ADDITIONS · Any of the following may be added at step 2.

— *Lemon* · zest of 1 lemon; also replace the simple syrup with a mixture of 120 g (½ cup) fresh lemon juice and 60g (½ cup) icing sugar.

— *Lavender* · 2 tsp dried culinary-grade lavender.

— *Vanilla Rose* · seeds from 1 vanilla bean, 1 tsp rose water.

— *Gingerbread* · 1½ tsp ground ginger, ½ tsp ground cinnamon, ¼ tsp ground cloves.

LONDON TEA·TIME *MUffins*

These muffins have always felt like a dessert to me. Jacob, our co-owner, head pastry chef, and creative mind in the kitchen, lived in London for a year, where he made these muffins to serve at afternoon high tea. The batter is good for up to five days in the fridge, so if you want to divide it to bake on different days, you can have fresh, tasty muffins twice in a week!

EQUIPMENT · You will need a stand mixer fitted with a paddle attachment and a 12-cavity muffin pan lined with muffin cup liners (we like tulip cups).

PROCEDURE · Preheat your oven to 350°F (180°C).

1. In a bowl, sift together the flour, baking powder, and salt. Set aside.

2. Place the butter and sugar in a stand mixer bowl and cream on medium-high speed until fluffy.

3. Turn the mixer down to low and gradually add the whole eggs and egg whites. Scrape down the sides of the bowl as needed. After the eggs have been added, turn the mixer up to medium and continue mixing for about 30 seconds more, until the butter and eggs are well incorporated and most of the lumps have disappeared.

4. Turn the mixer back down to low. Add the flour mixture in three parts alternating with the milk in two parts, beginning and ending with the dry mixture. Be sure to scrape down the bowl between each addition.

5. Remove the bowl from the mixer and fold in the white chocolate and lavender.

6. Using an ice cream scoop or a spoon, fill the muffin cups to about three-quarters full. Bake for 25 to 30 minutes, until a toothpick comes out clean or the centre of a muffin spring back to the touch. The tops of the muffins will still look light in colour.

STORAGE · These muffins will keep at room temperature for up to three days. The batter will keep in the refrigerator for up to five days.

INGREDIENTS

280 g (1¾ cups)	all-purpose flour
1 tsp	baking powder
1 tsp	salt
135 g (½ cup + 2 Tbsp)	unsalted butter, at room temperature
150 g (¾ cup)	sugar
2	large eggs
3	large egg whites
180 g (¾ cup)	whole milk
140 g (¾ cup)	white chocolate chips
2 Tbsp	dried culinary-grade lavender

raspberry pistachio
FINANCIERS

Like the madeleine, the financier is a small, spongy French tea cake whose recipe goes back to the late 19th century. Legend has it that financiers took on their rectangular shape in late nineteenth-century Paris to look like gold bars, appealing to bankers who wanted a quick, pleasurable breakfast without ending up with sticky fingers. They are made with ground almonds and beurre noisette—butter cooked until it turns a nutty golden brown. They lend themselves well to flavour additions, like our raspberry-pistachio pairing.

EQUIPMENT · You will need a financier mould. These are made of silicone or aluminum and come in a few different sizes. At Duchess, we use a 24-cavity, 1.5-oz rectangular silicone mould. If you can't find a financier mould, you can use a 24-cavity mini-muffin pan. If your mould is a different size, remember to adjust your baking time accordingly.

PROCEDURE · Butter and flour the mould or mini-muffin pan. Preheat your oven to 425°F (220°C).

INGREDIENTS

95 g (⅓ cup + 1 Tbsp)	unsalted butter
150 g (1¼ cups)	icing sugar
95 g (1 cup)	almond flour (finely ground almonds)
53 g (⅓ cup)	all-purpose flour
150 g (about 5)	large egg whites
1 tsp	vanilla extract or paste
1 pint (2 cups)	raspberries
30 g (¼ cup)	crushed pistachios

1. Make *beurre noisette* by melting the butter in a small saucepan over medium heat. Once fully melted, it will start to foam. Start whisking and continue to cook until the butter is a dark golden brown and has a nutty aroma. Pour into a heat-resistant bowl and set aside to cool.

2. Whisk together the icing sugar, almond flour, and all-purpose flour in a large bowl. Make a well in the centre of the mixture and pour in the egg whites and vanilla. Mix until well combined.

3. Add the cooled *beurre noisette* in two parts, whisking between each addition. Make sure to use a spatula to get it all out of the bowl as the dark brown sediment is loaded with a lovely nutty flavour that will make all the difference to your financiers.

CONTINUED ·

4. Place the financier mould on a flat baking sheet. Fill each cavity to about three-quarters full. For each financier, gently press a few raspberries halfway down into the batter. Finish with a sprinkling of crushed pistachios.

5. Bake for 10 to 12 minutes, until the financiers are a light golden brown on the sides and just baked on top. A proper financier has quite a soft centre so be sure not to overbake. Allow the financiers to cool slightly and gently pop them out of their moulds.

STORAGE · Financiers will keep at room temperature for up to three days. The batter will keep for up to three days in the refrigerator or up to one month in the freezer.

VARIATIONS

— *Blueberry & Coconut* · Replace the fresh raspberries with fresh blueberries and garnish with sweetened shredded coconut.

— *Earl Grey & Orange* · Using a mortar and pestle or a spice grinder, grind 1 tsp Earl Grey tea to a powder. Fold the ground tea, 1 tsp freshly grated orange zest, and 2 Tbsp orange marmalade into the batter.

BROWNIES

As far as brownies go, people tend to fall into two camps: fudgy or cakey. Cakey brownies tend to have some sort of frosting or icing, but here at Duchess, we prefer a rich, dense, fudgy brownie —no frosting required!

INGREDIENTS

160 g (1 cup)	all-purpose flour
¾ tsp	salt
1 Tbsp	cocoa powder
105 g (¾ cup)	dark chocolate
1 tsp	espresso powder *or*
2 tsp	instant coffee
170 g (¾ cup)	unsalted butter, at room temperature
250 g (1¼ cups)	granulated sugar
80 g (⅓ cup + 1 Tbsp)	firmly packed golden brown sugar
2 tsp	vanilla extract or paste
4	large eggs
66 g (⅓ cup)	milk chocolate chips
66 g (⅓ cup)	dark chocolate chips
55 g (⅓ cup)	chopped pecans

EQUIPMENT · You will need 1 × 9-by-9-inch cake pan.

INGREDIENT NOTES · We use Valrhona cocoa powder, Valrhona 64% Manjari callets for the dark chocolate, and Callebaut chocolate chips.

PROCEDURE · Preheat your oven to 350°F (180°C). Butter the cake pan.

1. In a bowl, whisk together the flour, salt, and cocoa powder. Set aside.

2. In a double boiler or a microwave on half power, slowly melt together the dark chocolate, espresso powder, and butter. Stir until smooth.

3. Add the granulated sugar, brown sugar, and vanilla to the melted chocolate and stir until combined. Allow the mixture to cool for 10 minutes.

4. Add the eggs two at a time, mixing until just combined. If you overmix the batter, your brownies won't be fudgy.

5. Gently stir in the flour mixture, milk chocolate chips, dark chocolate chips, and pecans until just combined. Pour the batter into the prepared pan.

6. Bake the brownies for 40 to 45 minutes, until shiny, cracking on top, and slightly pulling away from the sides of the pan. Using a toothpick, check if your brownies are done. It's normal for a few crumbs and chocolate to stick to the toothpick, but you should see no uncooked batter. If the toothpick comes out clean the brownies are likely overcooked and will be dry.

STORAGE · These brownies will keep at room temperature for up to five days.

PUMPKIN SPICE
Tulip Cups ——

When fall comes, we make these delectable muffins, among my all-time favourites. We enjoy them for a few months, and then they're gone again, leaving us all anticipating their return the next fall season. This perfect balance of pumpkin and warm spices will get you excited for Thanksgiving dinner.

EQUIPMENT · You will need a stand mixer fitted with a paddle attachment and a 12-cavity muffin pan lined with paper tulip cups or muffin liners. To frost the loaves, you may wish to use a piping bag fitted with a star tip (#826–#829).

PROCEDURE · Preheat your oven to 350°F (180°C).

1. In a bowl, whisk together the flour, baking soda, baking powder, salt, cinnamon, allspice, nutmeg, and cloves. Set aside.

2. In another bowl, whisk together the pumpkin purée, buttermilk, and vanilla. Set aside.

3. Place the butter and brown sugar in a stand mixer bowl and mix on medium speed for 1 to 2 minutes, until light and fluffy. Add the eggs one at a time, mixing well and scraping down the bowl between each addition.

4. Turn the mixer down to low and add the dry and wet mixtures, alternating three parts dry with two parts wet and beginning and ending with the dry. Scrape down the bowl between each addition.

5. Using an ice cream scoop or a spoon, fill the muffin cups to three-quarters full. Bake for 25 to 30 minutes, until a toothpick comes out clean.

6. Once the muffins are completely cool, frost them with a knife or pipe a large rosette of frosting on top of each muffin. Finish with a sprinkling of nutmeg.

STORAGE · Tulip cups will keep at room temperature for up to three days unfrosted or one day frosted. You can always keep the frosting in the refrigerator and frost the muffins as needed, bringing the frosting to room temperature first.

INGREDIENTS

240 g (2 cups)	cake flour
1 tsp	baking soda
¼ tsp	baking powder
¼ tsp	salt
½ tsp	ground cinnamon
¼ tsp	ground allspice
¼ tsp	ground nutmeg
pinch	ground cloves
220 g (1 cup)	fresh or canned pumpkin purée
120 g (½ cup)	buttermilk
1 tsp	vanilla extract or paste
113 g (½ cup)	unsalted butter, at room temperature
300 g (1½ cups)	firmly packed golden brown sugar
2	large eggs
1 batch	Cream Cheese Frosting (*page 113*)

CREAM·CHEESE
frosting

MAKES 2 CUPS

This is a versatile frosting that we use for our Hummingbird Loaves, Pumpkin Spice Tulip Cups, and Printemps Macaron Gâteaux. Feel free to use it to top any cake or quick bread. To give it extra flavour, we use a higher ratio of cream cheese to butter than most recipes call for.

EQUIPMENT · You will need a stand mixer fitted with a paddle attachment.

PROCEDURE · It's very important that your butter and cream cheese are at room temperature. If they aren't, you will end up with lumpy frosting.

1. Place the cream cheese and butter in the stand mixer bowl and whip on medium speed for 2 minutes.

2. Turn the mixer off and add half of the icing sugar. Mix on low speed until well combined. Repeat with the remaining icing sugar.

3. Add the vanilla, turn the mixer up to medium-high, and whip for another 30 seconds, or until light and fluffy. Scrape down the sides of the bowl as needed.

STORAGE · This frosting will keep for up to one week in the refrigerator.

INGREDIENTS

340 g (1½ cups)	cream cheese, at room temperature
168 g (¾ cup)	unsalted butter, at room temperature
120 g (1 cup)	sifted icing sugar
1 tsp	vanilla extract or paste

RASPBERRY *white·chocolate* SCONES

EQUIPMENT · You will need a baking sheet, a pastry cutter (optional), and a 3-inch round cookie cutter. If you use a smaller cookie cutter, make sure to decrease the baking time accordingly.

PROCEDURE · Preheat your oven to 375°F (190°C). Line the baking sheet with parchment paper.

1. In a large bowl, whisk together the flour, baking powder, baking soda, sugar, and salt.

2. Using a pastry cutter or two knives, cut the butter into the dry ingredients. You want your mixture to look quite dry with some small lumps of butter remaining. If you use a food processor, you run the risk of turning your mixture into a dough, and making it difficult to incorporate the buttermilk in step 3.

3. Make a well in the centre of the mixture and pour in half the buttermilk. Using your hands, incorporate the buttermilk by pushing dry mix from the bottom and sides to the centre while gently rubbing the mixture between your hands. Repeat with the remaining buttermilk until incorporated. The mixture should feel slightly dry—which will make for a flaky scone—but if it's so dry it won't hold together, add a few more tablespoons of buttermilk.

4. Add the raspberries and white chocolate chips and gently incorporate. If using frozen raspberries, make sure to work quickly to incorporate them before they thaw. Gently turn the dough onto a lightly floured surface (*Photo A*).

5. Press the dough together to form a large circle, about 1 inch thick (*Photo B*). Using a cookie cutter dipped in flour, cut scones out of the dough and place on the lined baking sheet about 2 inches apart (*Photo C*). Lightly sprinkle with sugar.

6. Bake for 25 to 30 minutes, until the scones are golden brown.

STORAGE · These scones will keep at room temperature for up to three days.

CONTINUED

INGREDIENTS

340 g (2 cups + 2 Tbsp)	all-purpose flour
1½ tsp	baking powder
½ tsp	baking soda
3 Tbsp	sugar
½ tsp	salt
130 g (½ cup + 1 Tbsp)	unsalted butter, cold, cubed
135 g (½ cup + 1 Tbsp)	buttermilk
75 g (½ cup)	fresh or frozen raspberries
100 g (½ cup)	white chocolate chips
	extra sugar, for finishing

VARIATIONS · Instead of the raspberries and white chocolate, you can use different combinations of fruit, nuts, chocolate, and flavourings. Here are some ideas.

— *Blueberry Lemon Glaze*
At step 4, add 105 g (½ cup) fresh or frozen blueberries and 1 tsp lemon zest.

To make the glaze, combine 120 g (½ cup) lemon juice, 120 g (1 cup) icing sugar, and 1 Tbsp water. Brush the glaze generously onto the baked scones while they are still warm.

The ideas below don't have any fresh fruit in them, so the dough will be a bit drier and will require an extra 60 g (¼ cup) buttermilk.

— *Cinnamon Raisin*
Add 1½ tsp ground cinnamon with the dry ingredients at step 1. Mix in 110 g (¾ cup) raisins at step 4.

— *Milk Chocolate Orange*
At step 4, add the zest of 1 orange and 150 g (¾ cup) milk chocolate chips.

— *Currant Ginger*
At step 4, add 1 tsp lemon zest, 80 g (½ cup) dried currants, and 70 g (½ cup) diced crystallized ginger.

— *Cheddar Pepper*
At step 1, decrease the sugar to 1 Tbsp and add 1 tsp ground black pepper. At step 4, add 100 g (1 cup) shredded cheddar cheese. Brush 75 g (⅓ cup) melted butter over the scones before baking instead of sprinkling with sugar.

Aunt Debbie's LAVENDER *· lemonade ·*

Jacob's Aunt Debbie is a hugely talented baker and gardener. A few years ago, she took a class on herbs that sparked in her the idea of creating a lavender lemonade—and the result was so fresh and different that we asked her for permission to use it at Duchess. Thanks to her, we now offer this lemonade through the hot summer months. I love it with a splash of gin.

The quality of the lavender that you use will make a big difference to your lemonade. Make sure your lavender is vibrant in colour and highly aromatic.

EQUIPMENT · You will need a small piece of cheesecloth.

PROCEDURE

1. Using a double layer of cheesecloth, tie the lavender into a sachet.

2. Combine the water and sugar in a saucepan and bring to a boil over medium heat. Stir briefly to dissolve the sugar.

3. Once boiled, remove from heat and add the lavender sachet. Let steep for about 15 minutes, applying pressure to the sachet with a wooden spoon to release the lavender flavour.

4. Remove the sachet and stir in the strained lemon juice. Allow to cool and then refrigerate. Serve cold with ice cubes.

STORAGE · This lemonade will keep in the refrigerator for up to a week.

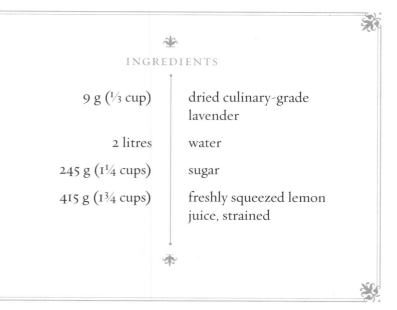

INGREDIENTS

9 g (⅓ cup)	dried culinary-grade lavender
2 litres	water
245 g (1¼ cups)	sugar
415 g (1¾ cups)	freshly squeezed lemon juice, strained

A VERRINE is an individually portioned layered dessert named after the small glass vessel in which it's served. The beautiful verrines created by today's pastry chefs take the humble homemade trifle to a new level of sophistication. When you are served a verrine, the transparency and vertical shape of the verrine glass not only allow you to appreciate the artistry of the dessert in all its parts, but also give you full control over the textures and tastes as you make your way through the layers.

As French verrine glasses can be difficult to find, we like to use 250-ml glass jars similar to jam or Mason jars: just add the lid and you have a wonderfully portable dessert! You can also use dessert glasses, drinking glasses, or even ramekins—although with ramekins you will lose the effect of the beautiful layers. You'll be sure to impress your guests with these refined little desserts. •

APPLE
Chocolate Mousse
VERRINE

MAKES 8 × 250-ML VERRINES

For this verrine, you can make the streusel, Joconde (almond sponge cake), and apple compote a day or two ahead of time, and make only the mousse at the time of assembly. Any verrine can be simplified by omitting layers if you are short on time or have dietary restrictions. For this verrine, for example, if you need a gluten-free and egg-free alternative, make only the mousse and the apple compote.

You will likely have leftover Joconde. It freezes really well and can be used at a later date for another verrine, or in a pinch, scoop some ice cream and fresh fruit on top for a nice dessert.

EQUIPMENT · You will need a stand mixer with the paddle and whisk attachments, a baking sheet, a 12 or 13-by-18-inch jelly roll pan, and an instant-read digital thermometer. You will also need verrines, dessert glasses, or clear 250-ml Mason jars. A large piping bag is also useful for filling the verrines as it allows you the control to keep the top and sides of the jar clean.

INGREDIENT NOTE · We use Valrhona 67% Ashanti callets for the dark chocolate in the chocolate mousse.

TO MAKE THE STREUSEL · Preheat your oven to 350°F (180°C). Line the baking sheet with parchment paper.

1. Mix the dry ingredients together in a bowl. Add the butter and, using your hands, work it into the dry mixture until clumps form. The dough will look slightly dry.

2. Spread out the streusel in small marble-sized chunks on the lined baking sheet. If any of the dough is dry, use your fingers to clump it together. Bake for 15 to 18 minutes, until golden brown. Set aside to cool.

CONTINUED

STREUSEL

1 Tbsp	packed golden brown sugar
¼ tsp	ground cinnamon
¼ tsp	ground ginger
50 g (⅓ cup)	all-purpose flour
40 g (3 Tbsp)	unsalted butter, at room temperature

JOCONDE SPONGE

112 g (1¼ cups)	almond flour (finely ground almonds)
112 g (1 cup)	icing sugar
3	large eggs
35 g (¼ cup)	all-purpose flour
3	large egg whites
15 g (1 Tbsp)	granulated sugar
20 g (1 Tbsp + 1 tsp)	unsalted butter, melted and cooled

APPLE COMPOTE

100 g (½ cup)	sugar
110 g (½ cup)	apple juice
3	medium Granny Smith apples, peeled, cored, and diced
½ tsp	ground nutmeg
1	cinnamon stick

TO MAKE THE JOCONDE SPONGE · Preheat your oven to 425°F (220°C). Line the jelly roll pan with parchment paper.

3. Using a stand mixer fitted with a paddle attachment, beat the almond flour, icing sugar, and whole eggs on medium-high speed for 8 minutes, or until almost doubled in volume.

4. Turn the mixer down to the lowest speed and slowly add the flour until just incorporated (*Photo A*).

5. In a separate mixer bowl, or using a hand mixer, whip the egg whites on medium speed until soft peaks form. Still mixing, slowly add the granulated sugar. Continue to whip until stiff peaks form (*Photo B*). The meringue is now ready.

6. Remove the bowl from the stand mixer. Add half the meringue to the batter, then half the melted butter, gently folding between each addition. Repeat with the remaining meringue and butter (*Photo C*).

7. Pour the batter into the lined jelly roll pan and spread it evenly using a long offset spatula (*Photo D*).

8. Bake for 10 minutes, or until slightly brown on top. Remove from the oven and let cool completely.

9. Once cooled, lightly sprinkle the top of the Joconde with sugar and flip it over onto a piece of parchment paper. Holding down the edge of the cake, gently peel off the parchment paper used during baking.

10. Using the rim of one of your verrine glasses or a round cookie cutter slightly smaller in diameter than your verrine glasses, cut 16 circles (2 per jar) out of the Joconde. These are now ready for assembly.

TO MAKE THE APPLE COMPOTE
(see 'Making a Caramel,' pages 271–272)

11. Heat the apple juice in a microwave or a small saucepan on the stove until scalding. Set aside and try to keep hot as you melt the sugar.

12. Place half of the sugar in a saucepan over medium heat. Gently melt the sugar by swirling it around the saucepan. Do not stir. Once the sugar is three-quarters melted, sprinkle the other half of the sugar into the saucepan. Continue to swirl until all the sugar is completely melted and has turned amber in colour (*Photo E*).

13. Slowly pour the hot apple juice into the melted sugar (*Photo F*). Be sure to pour slowly in a few parts, mixing between each addition, as the mixture will bubble up. If your sugar seizes up, don't panic! Using a heatproof spatula or a spoon, continue to stir until all the clumps have melted down. This may take a few minutes, so be patient. The colour will be a dark golden brown.

14. Add the apples, nutmeg, and cinnamon stick (*Photo G*). Continue to cook over low heat for about 20 minutes, stirring every few minutes, until the mixture is thick and the apples are really soft and slightly broken down (*Photo H*). Most of the liquid will have evaporated and the apples will be nicely caramelized. Remove the cinnamon stick and set aside to cool completely.

CONTINUED

CHOCOLATE MOUSSE

460 g (2 cups)	whipping cream
230 g (1 cup)	whipping cream
60 g (3 Tbsp)	glucose or white corn syrup
210 g (1½ cups)	dark chocolate

TO MAKE THE CHOCOLATE MOUSSE · The chocolate mousse should only be made when ready to assemble the verrines.

15. Fit your stand mixer with the whisk attachment and whip the 460 g (2 cups) measurement of the whipping cream on medium-low speed until soft peaks form. Set aside.

16. You will now need to make a ganache. Slowly melt the chocolate in a microwave on half power or over a double boiler.

17. In a small saucepan, heat the 230 g (1 cup) measure of whipping cream with the glucose until scalded. Pour the hot cream mixture over the melted chocolate in three parts. With each addition, mix with a spatula until smooth (*Photo I*). Continue to stir until the ganache has cooled to between 45° and 50°C (113° and 122°F) (*Photos J–K*).

18. Using a spatula, gently fold in the whipped cream in three parts, mixing until smooth with each addition (*Photo L*). Use the chocolate mousse immediately to assemble the verrines.

I *J* *K* *L*

TO ASSEMBLE THE VERRINES · Make sure the apple compote, streusel, and Joconde are completely cool before assembling the verrines.

19. Fill a large piping bag with the chocolate mousse and cut off the end (or use a spoon or ice cream scoop). Fill each jar with mousse to about one-quarter full (*Photo M*).

20. Top the mousse with a circle of Joconde and about ¼ cup apple compote (*Photo N*). Place another circle of Joconde snugly overtop.

21. Pipe more chocolate mousse on top until the verrine is nearly full (*Photo O*).

22. Serve at room temperature, garnishing with a sprinkling of streusel just before serving (*Photo P*). If not serving immediately, reserve the streusel and refrigerate the verrines, removing them from the refrigerator a half hour before topping them with streusel and serving.

STORAGE · Although verrines are best enjoyed the day they are assembled, they will keep in the refrigerator for up to three days.

BLACKBERRY GOAT-CHEESE *blancmange*

MAKES 8 SERVINGS

INGREDIENTS

1½ tsp	powdered gelatin
2 Tbsp	ice water
65 g (¼ cup)	whipping cream
110 g (½ cup + 1 Tbsp)	sugar
½	vanilla bean, sliced open lengthwise
35 g (1.5 oz, ¼ cup)	soft goat cheese, crumbled
480 g (2 cups)	buttermilk
65 g (¼ cup)	whipping cream
130 g (¾ cup)	fresh or frozen blackberries
1 Tbsp	icing sugar
¾ tsp	orange blossom water

When I was a little girl my Grand-mère often served us home-made blancmange, a cold, thickened dessert similar to pudding or custard. The basic ingredients of blancmange are usually cream and sugar. A friend brought us an updated version made with buttermilk and blackberries, and we took it to the next level by adding goat cheese. If you're not a fan of goat cheese, feel free to leave it out of the recipe.

EQUIPMENT · You will need 8 ramekins or small dessert bowls.

PROCEDURE · Keep in mind that the blancmange will need to set for at least 4 hours before serving.

1. Make sure the water is ice cold. Put it in a small microwavable bowl, sprinkle in the gelatin, and stir to dissolve. Set aside at room temperature until firmly set.

2. In a small saucepan, place the first measure of the whipping cream and the sugar. Using the back of a knife, scrape the seeds out of the vanilla bean into the saucepan. Place over medium heat, whisking constantly, until the sugar is dissolved.

3. Turn the heat down to low and whisk in the goat cheese until melted. Remove from heat. Briefly melt the set gelatin in the microwave, whisk it into the goat cheese mixture, and allow to cool for 5 minutes. Stir in the buttermilk and set aside.

CONTINUED

4. Using a whisk or a hand mixer, whip the second measure of whipping cream until soft peaks form. Be careful not to over-whip the cream, or your blancmange may turn out lumpy.

5. Using a spatula, gently fold the whipped cream into the goat cheese mixture.

6. Pour into the ramekins, leaving a bit of space at the top for the blackberry topping. Refrigerate for 4 hours, or until set.

7. Put the blackberries in a small bowl and crush them with a fork. Stir in the icing sugar and orange blossom water. Cover and refrigerate until ready to serve.

8. Just before serving, spoon the blackberry mixture into each ramekin to completely cover the blanc-mange. If desired, garnish with a whole blackberry and a twist of orange zest.

STORAGE · Blancmange will keep in the refrigerator for up to three days.

COOKIES

OATMEAL *Milk Chocolate* COOKIES

This cookie dough is very flexible and works well with all kinds of additions. At Duchess, we really like this milk chocolate version, but you could just as well add dried fruit, seeds, nuts, or spices to completely change this cookie—just let your imagination guide you. I love these cookies warm out of the oven with a cold glass of milk, and one just never seems to be enough!

INGREDIENTS

125 g (¾ cup)	all-purpose flour
½ tsp	ground cinnamon
½ tsp	baking soda
¼ tsp	salt
114 g (½ cup)	unsalted butter, at room temperature
110 g (½ cup)	firmly packed golden brown sugar
100 g (½ cup)	granulated sugar
1 tsp	vanilla extract or paste
1	large egg
150 g (1½ cups)	old-fashioned rolled oats
150 g (¾ cup)	milk chocolate chips

EQUIPMENT · You will need a baking sheet and a stand mixer fitted with a paddle attachment.

INGREDIENT NOTE · We use Callebaut milk chocolate chips.

PROCEDURE · Preheat your oven to 350°F (180°C). Line the baking sheet with parchment paper.

1. In a bowl, whisk together the flour, cinnamon, baking soda, and salt. Set aside.

2. Put the butter in a stand mixer bowl. Cream on medium speed for 2 minutes, or until light and fluffy.

3. Add the brown sugar, granulated sugar, and vanilla. Cream for another 2 minutes, or until smooth. Scrape down the sides of the bowl as needed.

4. Add the egg and mix until well incorporated. Turn the mixer down to low and add the flour mixture. Mix until just combined.

5. Scrape down the sides of the bowl. With the mixer still on low, add the rolled oats and milk chocolate chips. Mix until just combined.

6. Using an ice cream scoop, a spoon, or your hands, shape the dough into 2-inch balls. Place on the lined baking sheet 3 inches apart and flatten them to about 1 inch thick.

7. Bake for 13 to 15 minutes, until the cookies are lightly browned on the edges. Once baked, transfer to a cooling rack.

STORAGE · These cookies will keep at room temperature for up to five days.

DOUBLE GINGER
cookies

The ginger cookie is just loaded with potential, but when a recipe lacks in punch, the result can be such a letdown. At Duchess we have devised a ginger cookie recipe that's bold and positively pops with flavour and spice. I like my cookies to be quite spicy and emphasize the cloves, but there's no reason you can't alter the spice ratio to suit your own taste.

INGREDIENTS

225 g (1⅓ cups + 1 Tbsp)	all-purpose flour
½ tsp	baking soda
1 tsp	ground cinnamon
½ tsp	ground cloves
¼ tsp	ground nutmeg
¼ tsp	ground ginger
¼ tsp	salt
150 g (¾ cup)	firmly packed dark brown sugar
75 g (¼ cup)	fancy molasses
34 g (3 Tbsp)	vegetable oil
1	large egg
70 g (½ cup)	crystallized ginger, roughly chopped into 1-cm pieces
	granulated sugar, for finishing

EQUIPMENT · You will need two baking sheets and a stand mixer fitted with a paddle attachment.

PROCEDURE · Preheat your oven to 350°F (180°C). Line the baking sheets with parchment paper.

1. Sift together the flour, baking soda, spices, and salt. Set aside.

2. Place the brown sugar, molasses, and oil in a stand mixer bowl. Mix on medium speed for 5 minutes.

3. Turn the mixer down to low and add the egg. Mix for 1 minute.

4. With the mixer still on low, gradually add the sifted ingredients and mix until just combined. Add the crystallized ginger and mix until just combined.

5. Using an ice cream scoop, a spoon, or your hands, shape the dough into 2-inch balls and flatten with your hands to about ½ inch thick. Dip the cookies in granulated sugar and place on the lined baking sheets 3 inches apart.

6. Bake for 14 to 16 minutes, until the cookies are crackled on top and lightly browned on the edges. Once baked, transfer to a cooling rack.

STORAGE · These cookies will keep at room temperature for up to five days.

Grand-mère's
FLORENTINES

A florentine is a thin wafer-like Italian cookie made of caramel, nuts, and dried fruit. When I was living in Japan, I tasted this modified version and was instantly sold. It reminded me of a cookie that my grandmother used to make when I was little, which is why we called these Grand-mère's Florentines. With pastry crust underneath and plenty of caramel and almonds baked on top, you'll be addicted after your first one.

You can cut these cookies into any shape you like. At Duchess, we tend to make things round, but rectangles or randomly cut shapes would look quite lovely too. Of course, the 'scraps,' or 'florentine bits,' as we like to call them, make for wonderful bite-sized treats and should not be wasted!

EQUIPMENT · You will need a jelly roll pan, an instant-read digital thermometer, and a sturdy cookie cutter.

PROCEDURE · Preheat your oven to 375°F (190°C). Line the jelly roll pan with parchment paper.

INGREDIENTS

1 batch	Classic Pâte Sucrée (*page 184*)
100 g (⅓ cup)	honey
115 g (½ cup)	unsalted butter
125 g (½ cup)	whipping cream
200 g (1 cup)	sugar
120 g (½ cup)	water
2 tsp	white corn syrup
1 tsp	fleur de sel or salt
220 g (2¼ cups)	sliced almonds

1. On a lightly floured surface, roll out the pâte sucrée into a large rectangle about 1 cm thick. You want the dough to end up roughly the same shape as the jelly roll pan. Carefully roll the dough up onto the rolling pin and transfer it to the lined pan. Using a fork, poke the pastry all over to prevent air bubbles from forming as it bakes (*Photo A*). Bake for 12 to 14 minutes, until light golden brown around the edges. Remove from the oven and set aside.

2. Turn the oven up to 400°F (200°C).

3. In a small saucepan, heat the honey, butter, and cream until just scalding. Set aside and try to keep hot while you cook the sugar.

4. In a saucepan over medium heat, cook the sugar, water, and corn syrup until golden brown or amber in colour (*Photo B*) (*see 'Making a Caramel,' pages 271–272*).

CONTINUED

5. When the sugar has reached the desired colour, remove from heat and slowly pour in the hot cream mixture (*Photo C*). Be sure to pour slowly as the mixture will bubble up. Stir well using a heatproof spatula or a wooden spoon.

6. Place the mixture back over medium heat and cook, stirring occasionally, until it reaches between 120° and 125°C (250° and 255°F). Remove from heat and immediately stir in the fleur de sel and sliced almonds (*Photo D*).

7. Pour the hot caramel mixture over the baked sheet of pâte sucrée. Working quickly with an offset spatula or a heatproof spatula, spread the caramel evenly over the sheet, leaving a bit of room around the sides for the caramel to expand while baking (*Photo E*).

8. Bake for 8 to 10 minutes, or until the caramel at the centre of the sheet is bubbling.

9. Remove from the oven and allow to cool for about 15 minutes, until the caramel is slightly warm. Using a cookie cutter, cut out the florentines (*Photo F*). Cut the leftover scraps into bits for snacking on later.

STORAGE · Florentines will keep at room temperature for up to five days.

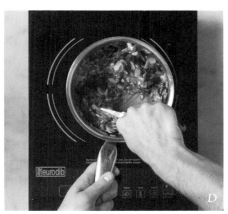

WHITE CHOCOLATE CHERRY PISTACHIO
—*cookies*—

INGREDIENTS

240 g (1½ cups)	all-purpose flour
½ tsp	baking soda
¾ tsp	baking powder
½ tsp	salt
140 g (⅔ cup)	unsalted butter, at room temperature
180 g (1 cup)	firmly packed golden brown sugar
1 tsp	vanilla extract or paste
1	large egg
65 g (⅓ cup)	white chocolate chips
42 g (⅓ cup)	roughly chopped unsalted pistachios
63 g (½ cup)	roughly chopped dried cherries

The sweet white chocolate paired with sour cherries and crunchy pistachios make this a wonderfully balanced cookie. This dough also makes a great base for old-fashioned chocolate chip cookies.

EQUIPMENT · You will need a stand mixer fitted with a paddle attachment and two baking sheets.

PROCEDURE · Preheat your oven to 350°F (175°C). Line the baking sheets with parchment paper.

1. In a bowl, whisk together the flour, baking soda, baking powder, and salt. Set aside.

2. Place the butter in a stand mixer bowl. Cream on medium speed for 2 minutes, or until light and fluffy, scraping down the sides of the bowl a few times.

3. Add the sugar and vanilla. Cream for another 2 minutes, or until smooth. Scrape down the sides of the bowl as needed.

4. Add the egg and mix until light and fluffy.

5. Turn the mixer down to low, add the flour mixture, and mix until just combined.

6. Remove the bowl from the mixer and gently fold in the white chocolate, pistachios, and dried cherries.

7. Using an ice cream scoop, a spoon, or your hands, shape the dough into 2-inch balls. Place the balls on the lined baking sheets 3 inches apart and flatten them to about 1 inch thick.

8. Bake for about 15 minutes, until the cookies are light golden brown and still a bit soft in the middle. Immediately transfer them to a cooling rack.

STORAGE · These cookies will keep at room temperature for up to five days.

VARIATIONS

— *Chocolate Chip* · Omit the white chocolate, pistachios, and dried cherries. Instead add 200 g (1 cup) chocolate chips (milk or dark).

— *White Chocolate Macadamia* · Omit the pistachios and dried cherries. Instead add 70 g (½ cup) chopped macadamia nuts.

dark chocolate MERINGUES

MAKES 12 LARGE OR 24 MINI MERINGUES

Despite my sweet tooth, I haven't always been a huge fan of meringues. Often, the texture seems rock-hard and they taste of sawdust. My feelings on meringues changed when I tried one with a soft centre in a tiny pastry shop in Paris. The outside was a bit crispy while the inside remained chewy and was deliciously filled with nuts and chocolate. It served as the inspiration for these meringues.

EQUIPMENT · You will need a baking sheet, an instant-read digital thermometer, a stand mixer fitted with a whisk attachment, and a large piping bag fitted with a large star tip (#828 or #829). Be sure all your chocolate pieces are cut small enough to fit through your piping tip.

INGREDIENT NOTE · We use 64% Valrhona Manjari chocolate callets.

PROCEDURE · Preheat your oven to 350°F (180°C). Line the baking sheet with parchment paper.

INGREDIENTS

120 g (about 4 large)	egg whites
230 g (2 cups)	icing sugar
¼ tsp	salt
2 tsp	vanilla extract or paste
70 g (½ cup)	dark chocolate, finely chopped

1. In a double boiler over medium heat, place the egg whites, icing sugar, and salt. Heat, whisking well every few minutes, until the mixture reaches 120°F (50°C).

2. Once the mixture has reached temperature, transfer it to a stand mixer bowl and whip on medium-high speed until stiff, shiny peaks form (*Photo A*), about 10 minutes.

3. Using a spatula, gently fold in the vanilla and chocolate (*Photo B*).

4. Insert your piping bag in a tall glass or container and fold the bag's sides down over the edge of the glass. Fill the bag with the meringue. Holding the bag perpendicular over the lined baking sheet, squeeze the mixture out while lifting the bag to form meringues 2 to 2½ inches wide (*Photo C*) (or 1½ inches wide for mini meringues). Leave about 2 inches of space between each meringue.

5. Bake for 18 minutes for larger meringues and 15 minutes for smaller ones. They should have grown a bit in size and be slightly cracked on top, but still look shiny and quite light in colour. If you overbake the meringues, they won't be soft in the centre.

6. Allow the meringues to cool on the baking sheet before removing them.

STORAGE · These meringues will keep at room temperature for up to two weeks. They do harden over time so fresher is better. Never store meringues in the refrigerator or freezer as those humid environments will cause them to go soft.

Duchess Bake Shop · 142

LAVENDER
shortbread

My friend Lara brought me this recipe when we first opened Duchess. With a few tweaks, we made it our definitive shortbread recipe, each month experimenting with new flavours. The inclusion of rice flour gives the cookie a wonderful texture and the dough freezes nicely if you want to save some for a rainy day.

EQUIPMENT · You will need a food processor and a baking sheet.

INGREDIENT NOTES · For most of our baking, we use butter with a high fat content (82% to 84%). Shortbread is one of the few exceptions because, while this butter is highly flavourful, it doesn't hold its shape very well. Instead, we use butter with a lower fat content (80%).

PROCEDURE · Preheat your oven to 275°F (135°C). Line the baking sheet with parchment paper.

1. Place the sugar, flours, and salt in a bowl and mix together. Add the cold cubed butter and, using your hands, toss until the butter is well coated.

2. Pulse the mixture along with the lavender in the food processor for 5 to 10 seconds, or until the texture becomes rice-like *(Photo A)*. Be careful not to over-process; at this stage the mixture will look dry and shouldn't come together as a dough.

3. Empty the pulsed mixture into a bowl and, using your hands, shape it firmly into a ball *(Photo B)*. The dough will seem quite dry and you may have to knead it to make it all come together.

4. On a lightly floured surface, roll the ball with your hands into an evenly shaped log about 2 inches in diameter *(Photo C)*. Wrap the log in plastic wrap and refrigerate it for at least 2 hours.

INGREDIENTS

100 g (½ cup)	berry sugar or superfine sugar
200 g (1¼ cups)	all-purpose flour
35 g (3 Tbsp)	rice flour
½ tsp	salt
226 g (1 cup)	unsalted butter, cold, cut into ½-inch cubes
2 tsp	dried culinary-grade lavender

CONTINUED

5. Remove the plastic wrap from the cookie log and, using a sharp knife, cut slices about 1 cm thick (*Photo D*). Place them about 1 inch apart on the lined baking sheet. Using a fork, poke the centre of each cookie to prevent air bubbles from forming during baking.

6. Bake the cookies for 40 to 45 minutes, until small bubbles form on top and the cookies are slightly golden. Immediately transfer to a cooling rack.

STORAGE · Shortbread will keep at room temperature for up to one week.

VARIATIONS · For plain shortbread, omit the lavender in step 2. You can also vary the flavour by substituting the lavender with other ingredients. Here are some suggestions.

— *Lemon Poppyseed* · Add 2 tsp poppyseeds and 1 tsp grated lemon zest.

— *Rosemary* · Add 2 tsp finely chopped fresh rosemary.

— *Earl Grey* · Add 2 tsp finely ground Earl Grey tea.

— *Cardamom and Orange* · Add 1 tsp ground cardamom and 1 tsp grated orange zest.

— *Toasted Almond* · Add 60 g (⅓ cup) roughly chopped toasted slivered almonds and ¼ tsp almond extract.

PIES

ALL ABOUT PIE DOUGH · Having
a good pie dough recipe is essential for any
baker's repertoire. It has so many uses—fruit
pies, buttertarts, galettes, quiche. I used to
be terrified of making pie dough. It seemed
like such a complicated procedure, and for
years I shied away from it. When I finally
tackled it, I found that it was actually quite
easy to master. I absolutely loved making
it and was proud of my pies' flaky crusts.
Over time I discovered that instead of
making it by hand, I could use a mixer and
achieve the same result.

There's always the debate as to whether
an all-butter pie crust is better. The butter
will give it really great flavour but it won't
be as flaky as if you had used shortening.
For our pie dough we use equal parts of both.
The dough retains that great buttery flavour
but also comes out nice and flaky. ◆

Easy Mixer
PIE DOUGH

This recipe will make more than you need for our pie recipes. You can easily halve this recipe to make exactly what you need for one pie, but because pie dough freezes so well, I always like to make the full recipe and keep the extra dough in my freezer ready to go for when I need to make a dessert in a pinch. All the pies in this chapter have been tested using a 9-inch pie plate (standard, not deep dish). If your pie plate is a different size, you may need to adjust baking times accordingly; for smaller pies, be careful not to overfill the shells.

EQUIPMENT · You will need a stand mixer fitted with a paddle attachment.

PROCEDURE

1. Place the flour, butter, shortening, and salt into a stand mixer bowl (*Photo A*). Mix on low speed until the fats are in small chunks and the mixture looks a bit dry (*Photo B*). This should only take 10 to 15 seconds. If you overmix you run the risk of turning your mixture into a dough, and then you'll have a difficult time incorporating all the water into it in the next step.

2. Add the ice water all at once and mix on medium speed until the dough just comes together (*Photo C*). Some small lumps of fat should remain in the dough.

3. Shape the dough into three balls (*Photo D*). Wrap each ball in plastic wrap and refrigerate for at least 30 minutes, making sure the dough is fully chilled before rolling out. At this point the dough can be frozen. Let it thaw completely before using it, but when you roll it out, be sure it's still cold.

STORAGE · Pie dough can be stored in the refrigerator for up to two days or in the freezer for up to six months.

PIE DOUGH

640 g (4 cups)	all-purpose flour
226 g (1 cup)	unsalted butter, in ½-inch cubes, cold
200 g (1 cup)	vegetable shortening, in ½-inch cubes, cold
1 tsp	salt
242 g (1 cup)	ice water

Tips & Tricks

MAKING PIE DOUGH · Here are a few simple tips for making the perfect pie dough:

- Use cold butter and shortening. When mixing the flour and fats together you want the fats to break down into small pieces but not totally disappear. This will be much easier to achieve if you make sure the fats are cold.

- Use ice-cold water.

- Don't overmix the dough. When you stop, you should still be able to see a few small lumps of fat and your dough should have a marbled appearance throughout. That's the secret to a flaky result!

BAKING A PIE · Here are a few simple tips for baking the perfect pie:

- When baking pies, always position your oven rack in the middle of the oven.

- Baking times may vary depending on your oven, the depth of your pie plate, and whether you're using disposable aluminum pie plates or glass/ceramic ones. All of our recipes are tested using glass pie plates, but even if that's what you're using too, you should use our baking times as a guideline only. Getting the perfect pie is really about checking the pastry during baking for the right colour. For a blind-baked shell, it should be a light golden brown; for covered and lattice-top pies, it should be a medium to darker golden brown.

- Make sure that you are generous with the egg wash when you brush it on before baking. This will give your pie an attractive top that's even, golden, and shiny. The same goes for the sugar: sprinkle it on generously and it will caramelize beautifully.

- Place pies directly on the oven rack for baking rather than on a tray. If you're concerned about dripping, place a piece of aluminum foil on the rack below.

- Be careful not to overfill pies that require blind-baked shells so that the filling doesn't boil over.

HOW TO ROLL OUT
· *pie dough* ·

1. Lightly flour your work surface and place the cold pie dough in the middle *(Photo A)*. Lightly flour the top of the dough and, using a rolling pin, roll the dough from the centre outward.

2. While rolling out your dough, keep rotating it, lightly flouring the surface under the dough as well as the top as needed to prevent it from sticking *(Photo B)*. Roll the dough out to about ½ cm thick.

3. Flip the pie plate you will be using upside down onto the dough. Using a sharp knife, trace a circle 1 to 2 inches out from the edge of the pie plate *(Photo C)*.

4. Fold the circle of dough in half and transfer it to the pie plate, making sure it's nicely centred *(Photo D)*. Unfold the dough, and then, using your fingers, gently press it down to form the pie shell, leaving the extra dough hanging over the edge of the pie plate.

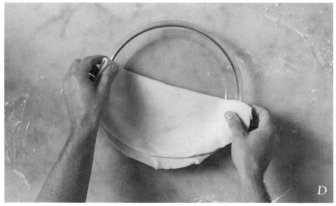

HOW TO MAKE
a blind-baked
· SHELL ·

Blind-baking a pie shell means that you are fully baking the shell before filling it. We like to do it for really juicy fillings (such as strawberry rhubarb) or custard fillings (such as pumpkin) to make sure the crust on the bottom comes out crispy rather than soggy. For a pie that doesn't need to be baked (such as banana cream), a blind-baked shell is a necessity.

1. Working around the entire edge of the shell, snugly tuck the dough under itself, forming a thick rim around the edge of the plate (*Photo A*).

2. Using the thumb of one hand, press the dough between the thumb and forefinger of the other hand, forming a crimped peak (*Photo B*). Continue around the entire edge. Freeze the shell for at least 15 minutes.

3. Remove the shell from the freezer and brush the edges generously with egg wash (1 egg white whisked with 1 Tbsp cream).

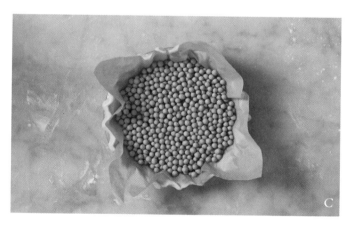

4. Cut a large circle out of parchment paper—large enough to cover the bottom and sides of the shell—and line the shell with it. Fill the lined shell to about one-third full with dried beans, rice, or pie weights (*Photo C*). This will help the shell hold its shape while it bakes.

5. Bake the shell at 375°F (190°C) for 30 to 35 minutes, until the edges are a light golden brown. Take it out of the oven and remove the parchment and weights. Using a fork, gently poke the bottom of the shell in a few places to make sure no air bubbles form (*Photo D*). Put it back in the oven for another 5 minutes to finish baking.

HOW TO MAKE
a covered pie ·

1. Cut out a second dough circle slightly larger than the first. Place your filling in the formed pie shell and lay the second circle overtop (*Photo A*).

2. Working around the entire edge of the pie, snugly tuck the dough under itself, forming a thick rim around the edge of the plate (*Photo B*). Make sure the edges are well pressed together to keep the filling from bubbling out during baking.

3. Using the thumb of one hand, press the dough between the thumb and forefinger of the other hand, forming a crimped peak (*Photo C*). Continue around the entire edge.

4. Brush the whole pie generously with egg wash (1 egg white whisked with 1 Tbsp cream). Using a sharp knife, cut eight short slits running outwards from the centre of the pie, or create your own pattern using short and long slits. These will act as vents for the pie to release steam while baking. Sprinkle generously with sugar (*Photo D*).

HOW TO MAKE
a lattice-top
· PIE ·

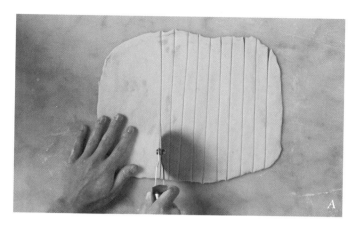

1. Fill the pie shell even with the rim (not heaping).

2. Cut eight strips out of the rolled-out dough, each one about 10 inches long and ½ inch wide (*Photo A*). Gently place them on top of the pie about 1 inch apart, lattice-style (four vertical and four horizontal), making sure they hang over the edges of the pie (*Photo B*). You can weave the strips if you wish.

3. Working around the entire edge of the pie, snugly tuck the dough under itself, forming a thick rim around the edge of the plate. Make sure the edges are well pressed together to keep the filling from bubbling out during baking.

4. Using the thumb of one hand, press the dough between the thumb and forefinger of the other hand, forming a crimped peak (*Photo C*). Continue around the entire edge.

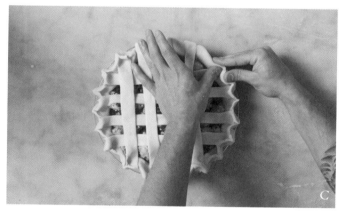

5. Brush the edges and lattice generously with egg wash (*Photo D*) (1 egg white whisked with 1 Tbsp cream) and sprinkle generously with sugar.

Apple Pie

MAKES 1 × 9-INCH PIE

This is our version of a classic apple pie. It's simple to make, yet so delicious and satisfying. When we first opened Duchess, I would sit on a chair at 2:00 am and meticulously peel, slice, and core each apple by hand. As we got busier, we needed to free up precious baking time in the early hours of the morning, so we switched to using a special apple peeler that peels, slices, and cores at the turn of a handle (found at most specialty kitchen stores). Not only has it been a huge time saver, it also cuts the apple slices evenly.

EQUIPMENT · You will need a 9-inch pie plate.

PROCEDURE · Preheat your oven to 375°F (190°C).

1. Peel, core, and slice the apples into 2-cm-thick pieces. Place the slices in a large bowl and toss with the lemon juice and lemon zest.

2. Place all the dry ingredients in a bowl and, using your hands or a whisk, mix well to combine.

3. Toss the dry mixture with the apples and set aside for 10 minutes, or until the sugar starts to dissolve.

4. Roll out the pie dough (*see page 152*). Fill the pie slightly heaping, dot with the butter pieces, and then cover and finish the pie as directed on page 154.

5. Bake the pie for 60 to 65 minutes, until the top is golden brown and the filling is bubbling through the vents. Serve warm out of the oven.

STORAGE · This pie will keep at room temperature for up to three days. It can be reheated in the oven before serving.

ASSEMBLY

1 batch	Easy Mixer Pie Dough (*page 150*)
2 Tbsp	unsalted butter, cut into small pieces

FILLING

about 6 large	Granny Smith apples
2 tsp	fresh lemon juice
1 tsp	fresh lemon zest
100 g (½ cup)	granulated sugar
145 g (¾ cup)	firmly packed brown sugar
30 g (3 Tbsp)	all-purpose flour
25 g (2 Tbsp)	cornstarch
¾ tsp	ground cinnamon
¼ tsp	salt

Sharileen's SOUR·CREAM CHERRY PIE

ASSEMBLY

1 batch	Easy Mixer Pie Dough (*page 150*)

FILLING

440 g (3½ cups)	fresh or frozen pitted sour cherries
175 g (¾ cup + 2 Tbsp)	sugar
40 g (¼ cup)	all-purpose flour
122 g (½ cup)	sour cream

One of my good friends, Sharileen, has worked for us at Duchess since the day we opened. She's a wonderful baker and I've always looked forward to her bringing in the lovely treats that she bakes at home. She brought us this delicious recipe for a cherry pie that uses the sour cherries that are commonly grown here in Alberta. Our opening week coincided with cherry-picking season and Sharileen brought in buckets of sour cherries that she had hand-picked from the tree in her yard. We labouriously hand-pitted each individual cherry to make into pies. To keep up with production, we've since switched to a supplier that provides us with good pre-pitted frozen sour cherries. If you have the time to pit fresh cherries, you will be rewarded with the best cherry pie out there.

EQUIPMENT · You will need a 9-inch pie plate.

PROCEDURE · Preheat your oven to 375°F (190°C).

1. In a medium bowl, mix together the cherries, sugar, and flour. Add the sour cream and stir until all the ingredients are combined. If your cherries are really juicy and look a bit watery, stir in another 2 tsp flour.

2. Roll out the pie dough and shape the shell (*see page 152*). Fill the pie with the filling (level, not heaping) and then cover and finish the pie as directed on page 155.

3. Bake for 70 to 75 minutes, until the top is golden brown and the filling is bubbling and thickened. Allow the pie to cool completely before serving.

STORAGE · This pie will keep at room temperature for up to three days.

maple
PECAN PIE

The maple syrup used in this pie really puts it in a class above your everyday pecan pie. This is the perfect pie for winter and great to make for the holiday season. Make sure you use good-quality maple syrup as this will affect the finished outcome of the pie.

ASSEMBLY

| 1 | blind-baked pie shell (*pages 150–153*) |

FILLING

60 g (⅓ cup)	all-purpose flour
165 g (¾ cup + 1 Tbsp)	firmly packed golden brown sugar
225 g (⅔ cup)	maple syrup
110 g (⅓ cup)	dark corn syrup
3	large eggs
90 g (⅓ cup)	sour cream
90 g (¼ cup + 2 Tbsp)	unsalted butter, melted and cooled
125 g (1¼ cups)	whole pecans

EQUIPMENT · You will need a stand mixer fitted with a whisk attachment.

PROCEDURE · Preheat your oven to 350°F (180°C).

1. In a small bowl, whisk together the flour and brown sugar, removing any lumps. Set aside.

2. Place the maple syrup, dark corn syrup, eggs, and sour cream in a stand mixer bowl. Using a whisk attachment, whip on medium speed for 3 minutes, or until the mixture is smooth and well blended.

3. Add the flour mixture and whip for 30 seconds.

4. Add the melted butter and whip for another 30 seconds.

5. Fill the pie shell until the filling reaches just under the rim of the pie. Be careful not to overfill as the filling will expand slightly in the oven and you don't want it to boil over. Arrange the pecans evenly over the top of the pie.

6. Bake for 55 to 60 minutes, until the pie is set in the centre. Allow to cool completely before serving.

STORAGE · This pie will keep at room temperature for up to four days.

lemon raspberry
MERINGUE PIE

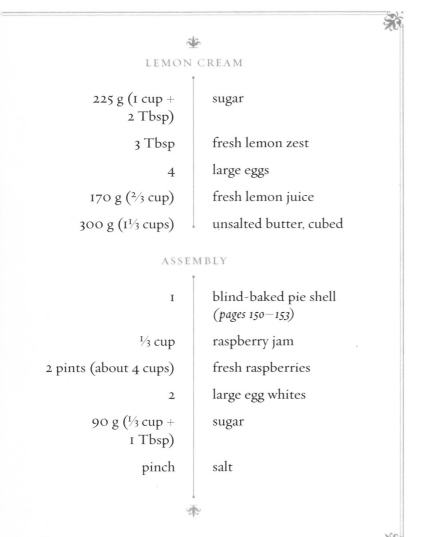

LEMON CREAM

225 g (1 cup + 2 Tbsp)	sugar
3 Tbsp	fresh lemon zest
4	large eggs
170 g (²⁄₃ cup)	fresh lemon juice
300 g (1⅓ cups)	unsalted butter, cubed

ASSEMBLY

1	blind-baked pie shell (*pages 150–153*)
⅓ cup	raspberry jam
2 pints (about 4 cups)	fresh raspberries
2	large egg whites
90 g (⅓ cup + 1 Tbsp)	sugar
pinch	salt

This is our special pie that we make for Father's Day—our twist on the traditional lemon meringue pie. The fresh raspberries, jam, and Duchess lemon cream make this a sellout every year.

EQUIPMENT · You will need a stand mixer fitted with a whisk attachment, a culinary torch, and a piping bag fitted with a decorative tip of your choice.

TO MAKE THE LEMON CREAM

1. In a bowl, rub the lemon zest into the sugar using your fingers. This will help bring the oils out of the zest. Add the eggs and whisk until combined, and then add the lemon juice and whisk again.

2. Transfer to a double boiler. Cook for 30 to 45 minutes, whisking and scraping down the sides every 10 minutes or so, until the mixture is thick and has darkened significantly in colour.

3. As soon as the lemon mixture has finished cooking, strain out the zest through a fine mesh strainer. Use the back of a spatula or a wooden spoon to try and get as much cream through the strainer as you can—you don't want to lose any of that great lemon flavour!

4. Gradually whisk the butter cubes into the strained lemon cream until the mixture is completely smooth and all the butter is incorporated. Or, use an immersion blender to blend in the butter; this will eliminate any graininess and leave you with velvety, extra-smooth lemon cream.

5. Cover the lemon cream and refrigerate for 3 to 4 hours, until set.

Make sure your blind-baked pie shell is completely cool before assembling the pie.

6. Using a spoon, spread half the lemon cream over the bottom of the shell. Arrange half the fresh raspberries overtop and spoon over the raspberry jam.

7. Spread the rest of the lemon cream overtop so that it's even with the rim of the shell.

8. To prepare the meringue, heat the egg whites, sugar, and salt in a stand mixer bowl fitted over a double boiler, whisking often, until the mixture reaches 130°F (55°C). Transfer the bowl to the stand mixer and whip on high until the meringue is shiny and forms stiff peaks.

9. The meringue must be piped onto the pie immediately after whipping or it will start to fall and lose its structure. Fill a piping bag with the meringue. Pipe one rosette in the centre of the pie. Around it, pipe a ring of rosettes, leaving a small gap.

10. Using a culinary torch, gently caramelize the meringue. Fill the gaps in the meringue with the remaining half of the raspberries. Refrigerate until ready to serve.

STORAGE · This pie will keep in the refrigerator for up to three days.

BANANA
cream pie

ASSEMBLY

1	blind-baked pie shell (*pages 150–153*)
double batch	Pastry Cream (*page 188, steps 1 to 7*)
4	ripe bananas
280 g (1¼ cups)	whipping cream
2 Tbsp	icing sugar
2 tsp	vanilla extract or paste

EQUIPMENT · You will need a stand mixer fitted with a whisk attachment and a piping bag fitted with a decorative tip of your choice.

PROCEDURE · Make sure your blind-baked pie shell and pastry cream are completely cool before assembling the pie.

1. Slice the bananas into pieces about ¼-inch thick.

2. Using a spoon, spread about a cup of pastry cream over the bottom of the pie shell. Arrange half of the sliced bananas overtop.

3. Spread about another cup of pastry cream over the bananas and top with the rest of the bananas. Add a final layer of pastry cream to fully cover the bananas, smoothing the top with a spoon or an offset spatula.

4. Place the whipping cream, icing sugar, and vanilla in a stand mixer bowl. Whip on medium-low speed until medium peaks form and the cream holds its shape when held up with a spoon.

5. Fill the piping bag with the whipped cream. Pipe the whipped cream on top of the pie in small rosettes. Refrigerate the pie until ready to serve.

STORAGE · This pie will keep in the refrigerator for up to three days.

PUMPKIN PIE

MAKES I × 9-INCH PIE

ASSEMBLY

I	blind-baked pie shell (*pages 150–153*)
	whipped cream, for topping (optional)

FILLING

110 g (⅔ cup)	firmly packed golden brown sugar
100 g (½ cup)	granulated sugar
2 Tbsp	all-purpose flour
½ tsp	ground cinnamon
¼ tsp	ground allspice
pinch	ground cloves
pinch	ground ginger
¼ tsp	salt
11 oz (1½ cups)	fresh or canned pumpkin purée
2	large eggs
3 Tbsp	fancy molasses
205 g (¾ cup + 2 Tbsp)	whipping cream

The popularity of our pumpkin pie at Thanksgiving has far surpassed any of our expectations. Our kitchen operates 24 hours a day for the week leading up to the holiday and we still can't make enough to satisfy the demand. This pumpkin pie is rich and creamy, with just the right amount of spices. It's a perfect ending to a turkey dinner.

PROCEDURE · Preheat your oven to 325°F (165°C).

1. In a bowl, whisk together all the dry ingredients.

2. In another bowl, whisk together the remaining ingredients. Add the dry ingredients and whisk until the filling is lump-free and well combined.

3. Fill the pie shell, leaving a bit of room at the top. Bake for 65 to 70 minutes, until the centre is set. Remove from the oven and allow to cool.

4. Keep the pie in the refrigerator until ready to serve. Top with whipped cream if desired.

STORAGE · This pie will keep in the refrigerator for up to three days.

FARMER'S
Saskatoon Pie

MAKES 1 × 9-INCH PIE

I remember spending summers picking saskatoons at the lake in Saskatchewan with my family. I would go home with my picking bucket nearly empty as I spent most of the time just eating berries off the bushes. Soon after we opened Duchess, a local farmer came in and told us about his saskatoon farm. I was thrilled to have found a great local supplier, so we quickly introduced this pie, which we have dedicated to Farmer Wade and Berry Ridge Orchards.

PROCEDURE · Preheat your oven to 375°F (190°C).

1. To make the crumb topping, in a bowl, combine the oats, flour, brown sugar, and cinnamon. Add the butter and, using your hands, work it into the dry ingredients until large clumps form. Set aside.

2. To make the filling, in a saucepan, combine the saskatoons, water, lemon juice, and sugar. Cook over medium heat until the sugar dissolves and the mixture begins to simmer. Stir in the remaining ingredients and continue to cook until the mixture thickens.

3. Fill the shell to the rim with the saskatoon filling and generously top with crumb topping.

4. Bake the pie for 45 to 50 minutes, until the top is golden brown and the filling is bubbling. Serve the pie slightly warm or let it cool completely.

STORAGE · This pie will keep at room temperature for up to three days.

ASSEMBLY

1	blind-baked pie shell (*pages 150–153*)

CRUMB TOPPING

45 g (½ cup)	old-fashioned rolled oats
55 g (⅓ cup)	all-purpose flour
55 g (⅓ cup)	firmly packed brown sugar
¼ tsp	ground cinnamon
55 g (¼ cup)	unsalted butter, at room temperature

FILLING

880 g (6 cups)	fresh or frozen saskatoons
3 Tbsp	water
3 Tbsp	fresh lemon juice
200 g (1 cup)	sugar
55 g (⅓ cup)	all-purpose flour
¼ tsp	ground nutmeg
1 Tbsp	cornstarch

VARIATION · *Saskatoon Raspberry*
Halve the recipe for saskatoon filling. Spread a layer of fresh raspberries over the bottom of the pie shell. Top with the saskatoon filling and the crumb and bake as instructed.

Pies · 167

STRAWBERRY
Rhubarb Pie

❧

ASSEMBLY

1	blind-baked pie shell (*pages 150–153*)

CRUMB TOPPING

45 g (½ cup)	old-fashioned rolled oats
55 g (⅓ cup)	all-purpose flour
55 g (⅓ cup)	firmly packed brown sugar
¼ tsp	ground cinnamon
55 g (¼ cup)	unsalted butter, at room temperature

FILLING

330 g (3 cups)	fresh or frozen rhubarb, cut into ½-inch pieces
200 g (1 cup)	sugar
30 g (3 Tbsp)	cornstarch
½ tsp	ground cinnamon
¼ tsp	ground nutmeg
¼ tsp	ground cardamom
1 Tbsp	fresh lemon juice
400 g (3 cups)	de-stemmed and quartered strawberries
¼ tsp	rose water

PROCEDURE · Preheat your oven to 375°F (190°C).

1. To make the crumb topping, in a bowl, combine the oats, flour, brown sugar, and cinnamon. Add the butter and, using your hands, work it into the dry ingredients until large clumps form. Set aside.

2. To make the filling, in a saucepan, place the rhubarb, sugar, cornstarch, cinnamon, nutmeg, cardamom, and lemon juice. Cook over medium heat until the rhubarb has broken down and the mixture is quite thick. This should take about 15 minutes. Remove from heat.

3. Stir in the strawberries and rose water.

4. Fill the shell to the rim with the rhubarb filling and generously top with crumb topping.

5. Bake the pie for 40 to 45 minutes, until the crumb is golden brown and the filling is bubbling. Serve the pie slightly warm or let it cool completely.

STORAGE · This pie will keep at room temperature for up to three days.

NECTARINE *wild blueberry* PIE

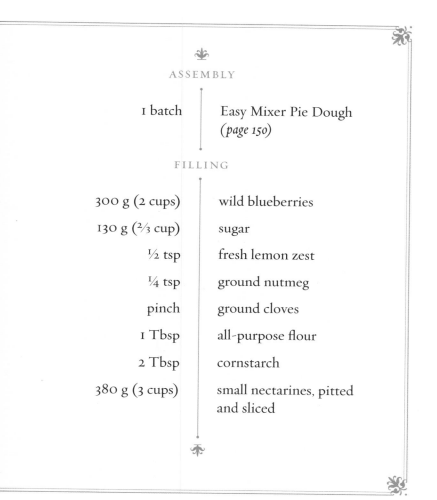

ASSEMBLY

1 batch	Easy Mixer Pie Dough (*page 150*)

FILLING

300 g (2 cups)	wild blueberries
130 g (⅔ cup)	sugar
½ tsp	fresh lemon zest
¼ tsp	ground nutmeg
pinch	ground cloves
1 Tbsp	all-purpose flour
2 Tbsp	cornstarch
380 g (3 cups)	small nectarines, pitted and sliced

When nectarines are in season we make sure to order caseloads from our fruit supplier in British Columbia and make as many of these pies as we can. If you can't get the smaller wild blueberries, regular-sized ones are just as nice.

EQUIPMENT · You will need a 9-inch pie plate.

PROCEDURE · Preheat your oven to 375°F (190°C).

1. In a saucepan, place the blueberries, sugar, lemon zest, nutmeg, cloves, flour, and cornstarch. Cook over medium heat, stirring occasionally, until the mixture has thickened. This should take 5 to 10 minutes. Remove from heat and fold in the nectarines.

2. Roll out the pie dough and shape the shell (*see page 152*). Fill the pie with the filling (level, not heaping) and then cover and finish the pie as directed on page 155.

3. Bake the pie for about 60 minutes, or until the top is golden brown and the filling is bubbling. Serve the pie slightly warm or let it cool completely.

STORAGE · This pie will keep at room temperature for up to three days.

Rhubarb Galettes

A galette is a hand-shaped pastry made with pie dough and a fruit or savoury filling. Almost any pie can be turned into a galette. These rhubarb galettes are one of our bestsellers. With the abundance of rhubarb in Alberta, it's easy to find an excuse to make these in the summer months. They can be served at room temperature or warm with a scoop of ice cream.

EQUIPMENT · You will need a baking sheet.

PROCEDURE · Preheat your oven to 375°F (190°C). Line the baking sheet with parchment paper right up to the edges, as the filling will bubble during baking.

1. To make the crumb topping, in a bowl, combine the oats, flour, brown sugar, and cinnamon. Add the butter and, using your hands, work it into the dry ingredients until large clumps form. Set aside.

2. In a separate bowl, place all the filling ingredients and toss to combine. Set aside.

3. Roll out the pie dough (*see page 152, steps 1 and 2*).

4. Using a small bowl or saucer (about 6 inches in diameter) as a guide, cut 6 circles out of the pie dough with a sharp knife (*Photo A*). You may need to re-roll the scraps to get all 6 circles. Arrange them on the lined baking sheet.

5. Place about ⅓ cup of the rhubarb filling in the centre of each circle (*Photo B*). Evenly distribute any sugar left in the bottom of the bowl over the rhubarb mounds.

ASSEMBLY

½ batch	Easy Mixer Pie Dough (*page 150*)
1	large egg white
1 Tbsp	cream

CRUMB TOPPING

25 g (¼ cup)	old-fashioned rolled oats
3 Tbsp	all-purpose flour
2 Tbsp	firmly packed brown sugar
pinch	ground cinnamon
2 Tbsp	unsalted butter, at room temperature

FILLING

300 g (3 cups)	fresh or frozen rhubarb, cut into ½-inch pieces
112 g (½ cup + 1 Tbsp)	sugar
3 tsp	cornstarch
½ tsp	ground cinnamon
½ tsp	ground ginger
pinch	salt

CONTINUED

6. For each galette, starting on one side, fold the pastry edge towards the middle. Do this around the galette, overlapping each edge, leaving a 1-inch space open at the top *(Photo C)*.

7. Whisk together the egg white and the cream to make egg wash and generously brush it over the galettes.

8. Gently press a small handful of crumb topping into the open centre of each galette *(Photo D)*.

9. Bake for 45 to 50 minutes, until the pastry is golden brown. Serve warm or at room temperature.

STORAGE · These galettes will keep at room temperature for up to three days.

Quiche LORRAINE

INGREDIENTS

1	blind-baked pie shell (deep-dish) *(pages 150–153)*
2 Tbsp	all-purpose flour
¾ tsp	salt
½ tsp	ground black pepper
½ tsp	ground nutmeg
3	large eggs
525 g (2¼ cups)	whipping cream
120 g (½ cup)	whole milk
210 g (1½ cups)	diced ham
100 g (1 cup)	shredded gruyère cheese

Jacob, our co-owner and head pastry chef, brought this recipe back with him from London, where he worked in a primarily French kitchen. It was there that he learned to make this exquisite quiche Lorraine. The secret is the cream-to-egg ratio and the hint of nutmeg that ties in all the flavours. The fillings are very flexible and you can use any combination of cheese, vegetables, and meat that you like.

At Duchess, we hand-shape the pie dough using a tall pastry ring to give our quiche high sides, but a pie plate is just as suitable. This recipe is designed for a deep-dish pie plate.

PROCEDURE · Preheat your oven to 375°F (190°C).

1. In a bowl, combine the flour, salt, pepper, and nutmeg. Add the eggs and whisk well, until most of the lumps have disappeared.

2. Add the whipping cream and milk and whisk until well combined.

3. Fill the blind-baked pie shell to three-quarters full with the custard. Sprinkle the ham and cheese over the custard.

4. Bake for 45 to 55 minutes, until the centre is just set (add 10 minutes if you're using a ceramic pie dish). If the outside crust starts to look dark while the quiche is baking, cover it with foil. The quiche is best eaten warm out of the oven.

STORAGE · Quiche will keep in the refrigerator for up to three days. Briefly reheat it in the oven before serving.

VARIATIONS · *Sundried Tomato and Leek* · Omit the gruyère and ham. Sauté 2 thinly sliced leeks in 1 Tbsp butter until soft. Remove from heat and toss in 1 cup thinly sliced sundried tomatoes packed in oil. Sprinkle this mixture over the custard in step 3.

Bacon and Mushroom · Omit the gruyère and ham. Fry 1 cup chopped bacon until crispy and remove it from the pan. Add 1½ cups chopped crimini mushrooms to the bacon fat and sauté until the mushrooms have softened. Sprinkle the bacon and mushrooms over the custard at step 3.

Courteau Family
TOURTIÈRE

INGREDIENTS

1 batch	Easy Mixer Pie Dough (*page 150*)
1 Tbsp	olive oil
455 g (1 lb)	lean ground pork
1	medium onion, finely chopped
1	celery stalk, finely diced
½ cup	finely chopped fresh parsley
1 tsp	salt
¼ tsp	ground black pepper
¼ tsp	ground cloves
¼ tsp	ground cinnamon
½ tsp	ground allspice
242 g (1 cup)	water or beef stock

In our family, food has always played an important part in all of our gatherings. We are proud of our French-Canadian roots and many of the dishes that we share together have been passed down through generations. Tourtière—French-Canadian meat pie—is the star of our réveillon (Christmas Eve) celebration.

Everyone always says that their mother's or grandmother's tourtière recipe is the best. Well, I've tasted many different tourtières and I really think that my mother's recipe is by far the juiciest and most flavourful. In the fall, she would visit her favourite butcher to buy the best quality pork and then go home and make up to twenty tourtières at a time to freeze to last us through the year.

When we first offered tourtière at the shop during the holiday season, we were surprised and overwhelmed by the number of orders we received. Many of our French-Canadian customers remembered tourtière from their childhoods, but over the years the recipe and tradition had been lost. I'm so happy to pass the Courteau family tourtière recipe on to you and hope that it will become a part of your family's holiday traditions.

EQUIPMENT · If you are planning to freeze your tourtière, use a disposable pie plate so that it can go straight from the freezer into the hot oven without fear of breaking the plate.

PROCEDURE · Preheat your oven to 375°F (190°C).

1. In a large frying pan over medium heat, heat the olive oil and sauté the pork, onion, and celery until the pork is cooked through.

2. Add the remaining ingredients and simmer for 15 to 20 minutes, until the liquid has reduced significantly but hasn't completely evaporated and all the flavours are well developed.

3. Roll out the pie dough (*see page 152*). Fill the pie, cover it, and finish it as directed on page 154. At this point, the tourtière may be wrapped and frozen unbaked.

4. Bake for 1¼ hours, or until the crust is golden brown. Or, if the tourtière was frozen, preheat your oven to 375°F (190°C), transfer the tourtière into it straight from the freezer, and bake for 1½ hours. Serve warm out of the oven.

STORAGE · Tourtière will keep frozen for up to six months.

ButterTarts

ASSEMBLY

1 batch	Easy Mixer Pie Dough (*page 150*)
¼ cup	Thompson raisins (optional)

FILLING

75 g (⅓ cup)	unsalted butter
145 g (¾ cup)	firmly packed golden brown sugar
120 g (⅓ cup)	golden or dark corn syrup
2	large eggs
1 tsp	vanilla extract or paste
¼ tsp	salt

When I'm feeling like a snack while working at Duchess, I often go for these. Flaky pie dough with a sweet, gooey centre… nothing beats an old-fashioned buttertart! I like mine with a few raisins, but feel free to leave them out if they aren't to your taste.

EQUIPMENT · You will need a 12-cavity muffin pan.

PROCEDURE · Preheat your oven to 375°F (190°C).

1. Melt the butter in a microwave for about 10 seconds, or until extremely soft and partially melted.

2. Place the sugar, corn syrup, eggs, vanilla, and salt in a bowl and whisk until smooth. Add the butter and whisk until smooth.

3. Roll out the pie dough (*see page 152, steps 1 and 2*). Cut out 12 circles, each about 2 inches wider in diameter than an individual muffin cavity (*Photo A*). You may need to re-roll the scraps to get all 12 circles.

4. Line each cavity with a circle, pressing it gently into shape. You can leave the sides smooth or shape them like a four-leaf clover for a more decorative edge (*Photo B*). Make sure the dough reaches the top of each muffin cavity to leave room for the filling to expand.

CONTINUED

5. Place a few raisins in the bottom of each cavity. Fill each cavity up halfway with filling (*Photo C*).

6. Bake for 20 to 25 minutes, until the centres have puffed up.

7. Let the buttertarts cool completely in the muffin pan. Once cool, use a sharp knife to run around the edge of each buttertart and gently lift them out of the pan.

STORAGE · These buttertarts will keep at room temperature for up to four days.

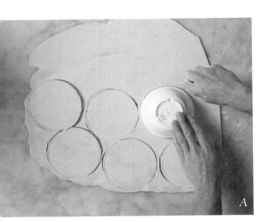

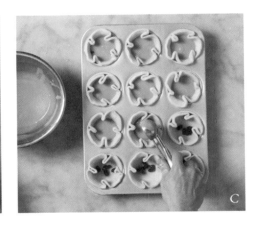

TARTs

ALL ABOUT TARTS · The shell used in French tarts is a sweet shortbread pastry known as pâte sucrée. A good classic pâte sucrée recipe is a necessity in any French pastry chef's repertoire. A tart can be filled with beautifully simple ingredients—such as whipped cream and fresh fruit—or something much more complicated and layered. Not only can pâte sucrée be shaped into classic tart shells, it also works great as a base for mousse cakes, bombe cakes, and even cookies.

I'm a bit of a purist and prefer to use the traditional French bottomless tart rings (flan rings) to shape the pâte sucrée. I love their straight sides, the sharp angle around their bottom edge, and how evenly the pâte sucrée bakes in them. To place the rolled-out pâte sucrée into the tart ring, we use a method called 'enfoncer.' This French word means to push or sink something downwards. Learning this technique can be a bit tricky at first, but once you get the hang of it, you'll really be pleased with the beauty of your tart shells. •

CLASSIC
pâte sucrée

Although most of the recipes in this chapter yield a single 8-inch tart, this pâte sucrée recipe will make enough dough for two tarts. Unbaked pâte sucrée freezes very well and you can keep the extra dough in the freezer ready to go for your next tart.

EQUIPMENT · You will need a stand mixer fitted with a paddle attachment, a baking sheet, and tart rings. We use 8-inch and 4-inch tart rings at Duchess. Unless otherwise noted, all of the recipes in this chapter have been tested with an 8-inch tart ring, but go ahead and use the smaller ones if you prefer. If using tart rings seems a bit tricky, you can stick with standard removable-bottom tart pans (they usually have a ruffled edge), though with these you may need to extend the baking time a bit.

INGREDIENTS

245 g (1½ cups)	all-purpose flour
75 g (⅔ cup)	icing sugar
35 g (⅓ cup)	almond flour (finely ground almonds)
¼ tsp	salt
145 g (⅔ cup)	unsalted butter, cubed, at room temperature
1	large egg
¼ tsp	vanilla extract or paste

TO MAKE THE PÂTE SUCRÉE

1. Sift the flour, icing sugar, almond flour, and salt together into a stand mixer bowl.

2. Fit the bowl on the stand mixer. Add the butter and mix on low speed until the mixture looks sandy (*Photo A*).

3. Add the egg and vanilla and continue to mix on low, stopping when the dough is barely mixed (*Photo B*). Some of the dry ingredients may still be visible. Be sure not to overmix or the dough will become tough and hard to work with.

4. Empty the dough out onto the counter and press it down by hand to work in the last of the dry ingredients (*Photo C*).

5. Shape the dough into two balls (*Photo D*). Wrap each ball well in plastic wrap and let rest in the refrigerator for 2 to 3 hours before rolling out. The dough will keep in the refrigerator for up to four days and in the freezer for up to two months.

VARIATION · *Chocolate Pâte Sucrée*
Follow the same procedure as for Classic Pâte Sucrée, substituting the almond flour with 3 Tbsp cocoa powder and increasing the quantity of icing sugar to 100 g (¾ cup + 1 Tbsp) and unsalted butter to 175 g (¾ cup).

TO ROLL OUT THE PÂTE SUCRÉE

6. Remove the pâte sucrée from the refrigerator and lightly flour a work surface and both sides of the dough.

7. Roll out the dough to about ½ cm thick, checking it often to ensure it's not sticking to your work surface. It helps to give the dough a 90-degree turn after each roll, flip it over frequently, and flour as needed (*Photo E*). As the dough gets thinner it becomes more delicate and difficult to flip over; just keep gently rotating it and lightly flouring it as you roll.

8. Place the tart ring on the rolled-out dough and cut a circle 1½ inches past the edge of the ring (*Photo F*). Gently move the circle of dough onto a large piece of parchment paper and transfer it to the refrigerator for about 15 minutes.

9. While the dough is chilling, prepare your tart ring. Grease the inside of the ring with a small amount of butter, making sure no bits of butter remain visible on the ring (*Photo G*).

CONTINUED

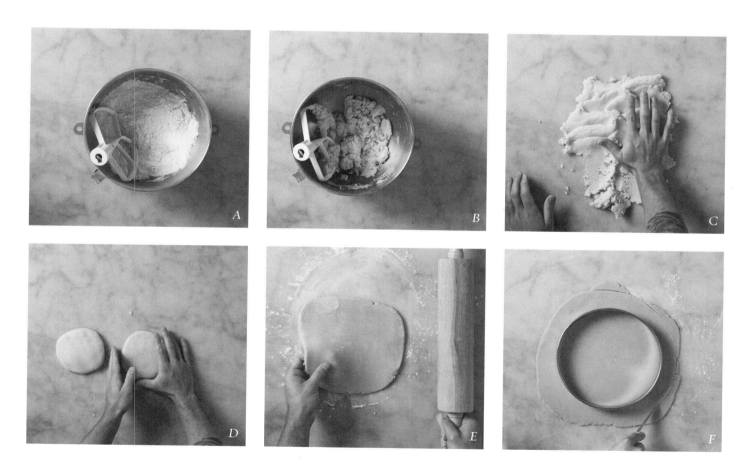

TO 'ENFONCER' THE DOUGH

10. Line a baking sheet with parchment paper and place the tart ring on it. Remove the dough circle from the refrigerator. Pick it up gently and centre it on the ring (*Photo H*).

11. Work the dough into the ring using your fingers to lift the edge of the dough and your thumbs to gently press it down into the mould. Work around all the edges until the dough is loosely positioned in the mould (*Photo I*). You may need to go around the ring in this way a few times.

12. Using your thumbs and taking your time, work the dough gently into the bottom edge of the ring, pressing it flat against the sides. Try your best to form a 90-degree angle along the bottom edge of the ring and make sure the dough is distributed evenly and doesn't get to thin (*Photo J*). If it's not well 'enfoncée,' you can end up with quite a shallow shell after it's baked, or holes, making it difficult to fill properly.

13. Run a sharp knife along the top rim of the ring to trim off the excess dough (*Photo K*).

14. Using a fork, lightly poke holes in the bottom of the shell so that no air bubbles form while baking (*Photo L*).

15. Refrigerate the shell for at least 15 minutes before baking.

TO BAKE THE TART SHELLS · Preheat your oven to 375°F (190°C).

– Tarts that will not be baked again once filled (such as fruit or lemon cream) will require a fully baked tart shell (*Photo N*). For an 8-inch tart, bake the shell for 18 minutes, or until the edges and base are a light golden brown. If using 4-inch tart rings, bake for 14 minutes.

– If you are making a tart that will be baked again after filling, your shell will need to be parbaked (partially baked) rather than fully baked (*Photo M*). In this case, reduce the baking time to 12 minutes for an 8-inch shell or to 8 minutes for 4-inch shells.

BRUSHING THE TART SHELLS · At Duchess we brush all of our fully baked tart shells with melted white chocolate to make the tarts more stable when filled. If you plan on making and serving the tart on the same day, this step isn't necessary, but if you'd like to serve the tart the next day or plan on having leftovers, coating the shell will prevent it from softening too much in the interim. Parbaked shells do not require this step, as they will be going back in the oven.

To brush your shell with white chocolate, make sure the shell is fully cooled. Slowly melt ¼ cup white chocolate in a microwave on half power or over a double boiler. Gently brush the white chocolate all over the inside of the shell, ensuring that you reach from the very bottom edge right up to the top edge (*Photo O*). Allow it to harden before filling your tart.

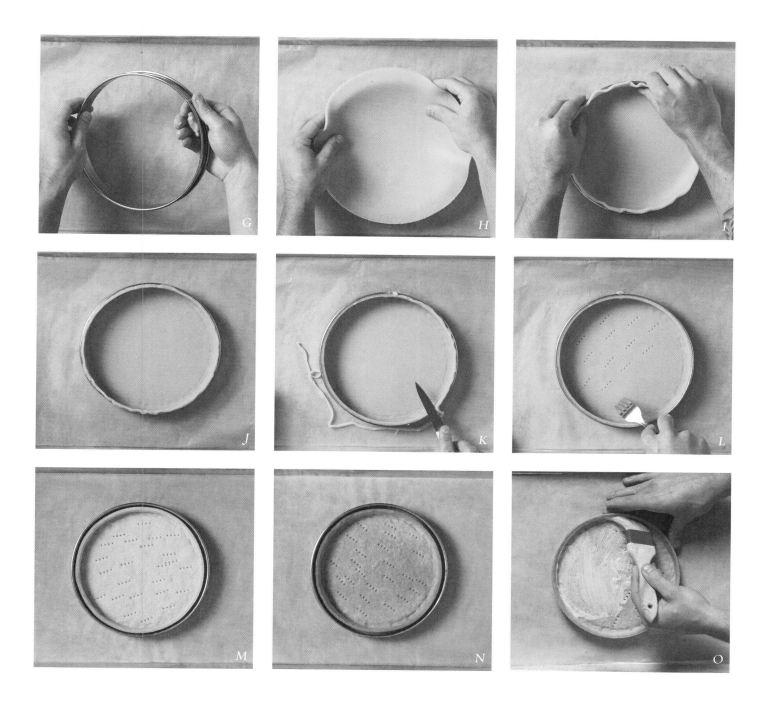

fruit TART

INGREDIENTS

1	fully baked tart shell (*pages 184—187*)

PASTRY CREAM

242 g (1 cup)	whole milk
1	vanilla bean, sliced open lengthwise
55 g (¼ cup + 1 tsp)	sugar
55 g (about 3 large)	egg yolks
15 g (1 Tbsp)	cornstarch
¼ tsp	salt
100 g (⅓ cup + 2 Tbsp)	unsalted butter, cubed

ASSEMBLY

	fresh fruit of your choice (we prefer berries)
¼ cup	apricot jam
1 tsp	water
	fresh lemon zest, for garnish (optional)

At Duchess, we only make fruit tarts for the few weeks a year when we can get our hands on freshly picked seasonal fruit. Sometimes we top the tart with just strawberries, while at other times we are lucky enough to be able to use a variety of different fruits that are all in season at once.

This recipe will make more pastry cream than you need. The leftovers are delicious on top of pancakes, served with fruit for dessert, or simply eaten with a spoon.

TO MAKE THE PASTRY CREAM

1. Heat the milk and vanilla bean in a saucepan until scalding.

2. While the milk is heating, place the sugar and egg yolks in a bowl and whisk until the yolks have lightened in colour. This will take a few minutes of vigorous whisking. Whisk in the cornstarch and salt.

3. Remove the vanilla bean from the heated milk and, using the back of a knife, scrape the seeds back into the milk.

4. Slowly drizzle the hot milk into the yolk mixture while continuing to whisk. If you add the hot milk too quickly the eggs will curdle and your pastry cream will come out lumpy.

5. Once all the milk has been added, transfer the mixture back to the saucepan and place over medium heat. Whisking constantly, bring the mixture to a boil, and continue cooking for 5 minutes more, whisking the entire time.

6. Remove from heat. Immediately strain the pastry cream through a fine mesh strainer to remove any lumps. Add the butter and whisk until smooth; or, if you want your pastry cream even smoother, use an immersion blender.

7. Cover the pastry cream and refrigerate for 2 to 3 hours, until set.

TO ASSEMBLE THE TART

8. Use a spatula to slightly break up the cold pastry cream. Fill the tart shell with pastry cream to just slightly below the rim, spreading it out smoothly with a knife or a small offset spatula.

9. Arrange the fresh berries or other fruit in a pattern on top.

10. In a microwave or over the stove, gently melt the apricot jam with the water—without letting it come to a boil—and brush it generously over the top of the fruit. Garnish with fresh lemon zest. If not serving immediately, refrigerate until ready to serve.

STORAGE · This fruit tart will keep in the refrigerator for up to three days.

peach · lavender
FINANCIER TART

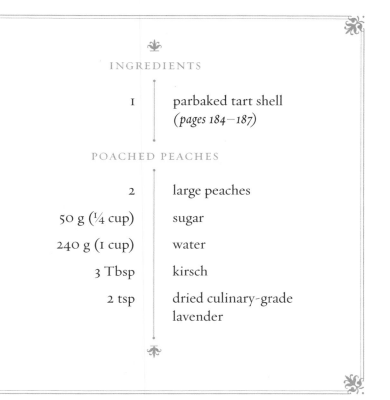

INGREDIENTS

| I | parbaked tart shell *(pages 184–187)* |

POACHED PEACHES

2	large peaches
50 g (¼ cup)	sugar
240 g (1 cup)	water
3 Tbsp	kirsch
2 tsp	dried culinary-grade lavender

This tart is best made later in summer when free-stone peaches are in season. We poach the peaches in kirsch and lavender. The peaches need to soak for at least eight hours in the poaching syrup, so be sure to consider this when planning when to bake the tart. I like to poach extra peaches to serve as a dessert on their own or warm over vanilla ice cream.

TO PREPARE THE POACHED PEACHES

1. In a saucepan, put about 4 cups of water on to boil. The saucepan needs to be small enough for the water to cover the peaches.

2. Using a sharp knife, score a cross on the bottom of each peach. This will give you a starting point for peeling after blanching.

3. Blanch the peaches in the boiling water for 2 minutes. Plunge them into ice-cold water and allow them to cool slightly. Remove them from the water, peel, pit, and slice into quarters.

4. To make the syrup, combine the sugar and water in a small saucepan. Bring to a boil, stir in the kirsch and lavender, and remove from heat.

5. Pour the syrup over the prepared peaches and leave them in the refrigerator to soak for at least 8 hours.

CONTINUED

FINANCIER BATTER

50 g (¼ cup)	unsalted butter
90 g (¾ cup)	icing sugar
33 g (⅓ cup)	almond flour (finely ground almonds)
40 g (¼ cup)	all-purpose flour
pinch	baking powder
3	large egg whites
¼ tsp	vanilla extract or paste
I tsp	dried culinary-grade lavender

FINISHING

I Tbsp	peach jam
	dried culinary-grade lavender, for garnish

TO MAKE THE FINANCIER BATTER

6. When the peaches have finished poaching, make *beurre noisette* by melting the butter in a small saucepan over medium heat. Once it's fully melted, it will start to foam. Start whisking, and continue to cook until the butter is a dark golden brown and has a nutty aroma. Pour into a heat-resistant bowl and set aside to cool.

7. In a large bowl, whisk together the icing sugar, almond flour, all-purpose flour, and baking powder. Make a well in the centre and add in the egg whites, vanilla, and lavender. Mix until well combined.

8. Add the cooled *beurre noisette* in two parts, whisking between each addition. Be sure to use a spatula to get it all out of the bowl as the dark brown sediment is loaded with a lovely nutty flavour that will make all the difference to your tart.

9. Using a small offset spatula, gently spread the financier batter over the bottom of the tart shell, taking care not to break it. The batter should fill the shell up about halfway. Be careful to not overfill, as the batter will rise in the oven (there may be a bit left over).

TO BAKE AND FINISH THE TART · Preheat your oven to 375°F (190°C).

10. Remove the peaches from the poaching syrup and place them on a paper towel to absorb any excess syrup. Reserve 2 Tbsp of the poaching syrup to use in the finishing glaze. Gently press the peaches into the financier batter in a circular pattern.

11. Bake the tart for 30 to 35 minutes, until it has puffed up nicely and is golden brown.

12. In a microwave or over the stove, gently melt the peach jam together with 2 Tbsp of the reserved poaching syrup, without letting it boil. Brush the mixture generously over the tart. Sprinkle with lavender.

STORAGE · This fruit tart will keep in the refrigerator for up to three days.

CLASSIC
chocolate TART

This classic chocolate tart is quite simple to make and will win over any chocolate lover. The added layer of feuilletine (caramelized cereal flakes), the creaminess of the ganache, and the subtle character of the chocolate give the tart a deep and complex flavour.

The quality of the chocolate you use really counts in this recipe, so do splurge on the best chocolate you can afford rather than using standard grocery store chocolate chips.

INGREDIENT NOTES · In the feuilletine base we use Valrhona 66% Caraïbe callets. In the chocolate ganache we use Valrhona 64% Manjari callets and Valrhona 40% Jivara callets.

ASSEMBLY

1	fully baked chocolate tart shell *(pages 184–187)*
75 g (½ cup)	dark chocolate
38 g (⅓ cup)	feuilletine
	cocoa nibs, for garnish (optional)

CHOCOLATE GANACHE

92 g (⅔ cup)	dark chocolate
106 g (¾ cup)	milk chocolate
172 g (¾ cup)	whipping cream
3 tsp	white corn syrup
24 g (2 Tbsp)	unsalted butter

TO MAKE THE FEUILLETINE BASE

1. Slowly melt the 75 g (½ cup) measurement of dark chocolate over a double boiler or in a microwave. Once the chocolate is fully melted, mix in the feuilletine *(Photos A–B, page 204)*.

2. Using an offset spatula, gently press the mixture into the bottom of the tart shell, making sure to fill all the corners *(Photo C, page 204)*. Set aside.

TO MAKE THE CHOCOLATE GANACHE

3. Slowly melt the dark and milk chocolate for the ganache over a double boiler or in a microwave.

4. While the chocolate is melting, combine the cream and corn syrup in a saucepan and heat until just scalding.

5. Pour the hot cream over the chocolate in three parts, using a spatula to mix well between each addition.

6. Add the butter in a few small pieces and, using a spatula, mix until smooth and no traces of butter remain.

TO FINISH THE TART

7. Pour the ganache into the tart shell, making sure not to overfill it (there may be a bit left over). Sprinkle cocoa nibs in a decorative line over the top of the tart for added crunch.

8. Refrigerate the tart for at least 3 hours, until well set. Remove from the refrigerator about 30 minutes before serving.

STORAGE · This tart will keep in the refrigerator for up to three days. ·

Autumn Tart

INGREDIENTS

1	parbaked tart shell (*pages 184–187*)
¼ cup	hazelnuts, roughly chopped, for garnish

CANDIED ORANGE SLICES

1	medium orange (not peeled)
200 g (1 cup)	sugar
240 g (1 cup)	water
½	vanilla bean, sliced open lengthwise
pinch	ground cloves *or*
1	whole clove
pinch	ground nutmeg
pinch	ground cinnamon
8	peppercorns

Autumn is my favourite season, and I can't think of a better way to mark it than with a tart that is not only beautiful in colour but also steeped in wonderful spices and comforting caramel. This is a great alternative to a pumpkin pie for Thanksgiving dinner.

EQUIPMENT · You will need a stand mixer fitted with a whisk attachment.

TO PREPARE THE ORANGE SLICES · Prepare a *cartouche* —a paper lid to keep the oranges submerged in the syrup while they are poaching. Do this by cutting a circle out of parchment paper sized to just fit inside a small saucepan. Make a small hole in the centre for venting.

1. Slice the orange as thinly as possible while keeping the fruit intact.

2. In a small saucepan, combine the sugar, water, vanilla bean, and spices. Bring to a boil.

3. Reduce the heat to minimum and lay the orange slices in the syrup so that they overlap and form a circle (*Photo A*). Fit the *cartouche* snugly overtop (*Photo B*). Simmer on low for 2 hours, or until the orange slices are soft, have absorbed some of the syrup, and look slightly translucent. To keep the delicate orange slices from falling apart, make sure the simmering temperature is as low as possible and your syrup does not boil.

4. Remove from heat and let cool. Cover the saucepan and refrigerate overnight.

CONTINUED

FRANGIPANE

40 g (⅓ cup)	almond flour (finely ground almonds)
2 Tbsp	all-purpose flour
	zest of 1 orange
40 g (⅓ cup)	finely chopped hazelnuts
1	large egg
3 Tbsp	berry or superfine sugar
55 g (¼ cup)	unsalted butter, melted
1 Tbsp	sour cream

CARAMEL GLAZE

1 Tbsp	ice water
½ tsp	powdered gelatin
90 g (⅓ cup + 1 Tbsp)	whipping cream
100 g (½ cup)	berry or superfine sugar
1 Tbsp	unsalted butter

TO MAKE THE FRANGIPANE · Preheat your oven to 375°F (190°C).

5. In a bowl, mix together the almond flour, all-purpose flour, orange zest, and hazelnuts. Set aside.

6. Put the egg and sugar in a stand mixer bowl and whisk on medium speed until frothy. Slowly stream in the melted butter and mix until well incorporated.

7. Remove the bowl from the mixer and gently fold in the dry ingredients and the sour cream until just combined.

8. Using a small offset spatula, gently spread the frangipane batter over the bottom of the tart, taking care not to break the shell. The batter should fill up the tart about halfway. Be careful not to overfill, as the frangipane will rise in the oven (there may be a bit left over).

9. Bake for 18 to 20 minutes, until the frangipane is golden brown and has puffed up. Prepare the caramel glaze while the frangipane is in the oven.

TO MAKE THE CARAMEL GLAZE
(see 'Making a Caramel,' pages 271–272)

10. Make sure the water is ice cold. Put it in a small microwavable bowl, sprinkle in the gelatin, and stir to dissolve. Set aside at room temperature until firmly set.

11. Heat the cream in a microwave or a small saucepan on the stove until scalding. Set aside as you melt the sugar.

12. Place about a quarter of the sugar in a saucepan over medium heat. Gently melt the sugar, swirling the saucepan around as needed. Do not stir. Once the sugar is almost melted, sprinkle another quarter of the sugar into the saucepan and continue to swirl. Repeat twice more and cook until all the sugar is completely melted and has turned amber in colour.

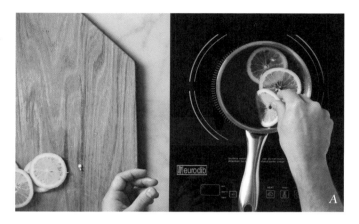

13. Remove from heat and slowly pour in the hot cream. Be sure to pour carefully as the mixture will bubble up. Using a heatproof spatula or a wooden spoon, mix the caramel until smooth. Using a fine mesh strainer, immediately strain the caramel into a heat-proof bowl.

14. Mix the butter into the caramel until it is fully melted and well incorporated.

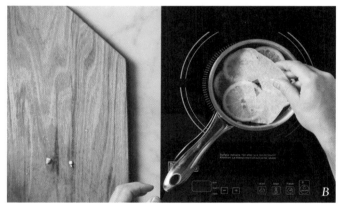

15. Briefly melt the set gelatin in the microwave and stir it into the caramel. Set aside and let cool slightly.

TO FINISH THE TART

16. Brush the baked frangipane generously with orange poaching syrup.

17. Pour on a layer of caramel. Refrigerate until set.

18. When the caramel is set, gently remove the orange slices from the syrup. They will be quite soft so be careful not to tear them. Using a paper towel, pat the excess syrup off the slices (*Photo C*) and arrange them over the caramel. Sprinkle with chopped hazelnuts to finish. Serve at room temperature.

STORAGE · This tart will keep at room temperature for up to three days.

LEMON
cream TART

MAKES 1 × 8-INCH TART

This is our version of a classic lemon tart. Rather than using lemon curd, which is usually made with egg yolks and cornstarch, we prefer to use lemon cream, which uses whole eggs and more butter. This recipe will require two or three lemons depending on their size.

When we make lemon cream in a large batch at Duchess, we use about 250 lemons, all of which we zest by hand before putting them through the juicer. It takes about five and a half hours to cook the cream, during which time we stir it every half hour. Not a task for the faint of heart!

ASSEMBLY

1	fully baked tart shell (*pages 184–187*)
	a few fresh berries, for garnish
	icing sugar, for garnish

LEMON CREAM

112 g (½ cup + 1 Tbsp)	sugar
1½ Tbsp	fresh lemon zest
2	large eggs
85 g (⅓ cup)	fresh lemon juice
150 g (⅔ cup)	unsalted butter, cubed

TO MAKE THE LEMON CREAM

1. In a bowl, rub the lemon zest into the sugar using your fingers. This will help bring the oils out of the zest. Add the eggs and whisk until combined. Add the lemon juice and whisk again.

2. Transfer to a double boiler. Cook for 30 to 45 minutes, whisking and scraping down the sides every 10 minutes or so, until the mixture is thick and has darkened significantly in colour.

3. As soon as the lemon mixture has finished cooking, strain out the zest through a fine mesh strainer. Use the back of a spatula or a wooden spoon to push as much cream through the strainer as you can—you don't want to lose any of that great lemon flavour!

Duchess Bake Shop · 198

4. Gradually whisk the butter cubes into the strained lemon cream until the mixture is completely smooth and all the butter is incorporated. Alternately, use an immersion blender to blend in the butter; this will eliminate any graininess and leave you with velvety, extra-smooth lemon cream.

5. Cover the lemon cream and refrigerate for 3 to 4 hours, until set.

TO FILL THE TART

6. Remove the lemon cream from the refrigerator and mix it vigorously with a spatula to soften it up. This will give your tart a really smooth finish. You can tell you've mixed it enough when a stream poured out slowly disappears back into itself. Once you have the lemon cream at the desired texture, slowly pour it into the shell, stopping just below the rim. Be sure not to overfill the shell.

7. Return the tart to the refrigerator and chill until set, about 45 minutes. Garnish with a few fresh berries and a dusting of icing sugar.

STORAGE · This tart will keep in the refrigerator for up to three days.

KEY LIME TART

MAKES 4 / 4-INCH TARTS

Soon after we opened Duchess, we accidentally got delivered a case of limes. We had to come up with a way to use them up—and our Key Lime Tart was born. This tart is creamy and smooth, with just the right balance of tart and sweet. If you can get your hands on real Key limes that's great, though regular limes will also do the trick. Don't hesitate to use the full amount of zest the recipe calls for: this is where the tart really gets its flavour!

To give the classic Key lime pie a modern look, we hand-shape the crusts in rings and remove the rings after baking. You can also pack the crust mixture into mini tart shells or a standard 8-inch pie pan, as with any crumb crust.

CRUST

165 g (1¼ cups)	graham crumbs
36 g (3 Tbsp)	sugar
105 g (½ cup)	unsalted butter, melted

FILLING

2	large egg yolks
1 Tbsp	firmly packed grated lime zest (about 4 limes)
300 ml (1¼ cups)	sweetened condensed milk
115 g (½ cup)	fresh lime juice (about 4 limes)

EQUIPMENT · You will need 4 × 4-inch tart or pastry rings, 1 to 1½ inches high. Alternately, use mini tart shells or an 8-inch pie plate. You will also need a baking sheet.

PROCEDURE · Preheat your oven to 300°F (150°C). Line the baking sheet with parchment paper and arrange the tart rings on it.

1. In a bowl, combine the graham crumbs, sugar, and butter. Stir until the graham crumbs are moist and stick together slightly when clumped.

2. Place about ½ cup of the crumb mixture into one of the rings. Using your fingers, gently press crumbs up the sides of the ring to cover. Fill in the bottom with the crumbs that remain. Repeat for the remaining rings. If you're using a pie plate, lightly butter the plate and press the crumbs evenly along the bottom and sides using your fingers.

3. Bake the tart shells for 12 minutes (14 minutes if using a pie plate). Remove from the oven and increase the oven's temperature to 325°F (160°C).

4. To make the filling, whisk together the egg yolks, lime zest, and condensed milk in a bowl until smooth. Slowly pour in the lime juice and whisk again until smooth.

5. Using an ice cream scoop or a large spoon, fill the baked tart shells level with the top.

6. Bake the tarts for 10 minutes (18 minutes if using a pie plate). Allow them to cool for 10 minutes before gently removing the tart rings. Refrigerate for at least 2 hours, until fully chilled. Using a pie server or a large spatula, transfer the chilled tarts to individual plates or small cake boards and serve.

STORAGE · Key lime tarts will keep in the refrigerator for up to four days.

TART
MONTRÉAL

Although I love a traditional chocolate tart, the French-Canadian in me can't resist this modified version, which includes maple syrup. If you can't find the feuilletine (caramelized cereal flakes) this recipe calls for, you can omit the feuilletine base, though for me that layer of crunch is what really brings everything together.

For this tart, don't skimp on the quality of the maple syrup or bourbon, as doing so will definitely affect the end result. The spiced whipped ganache needs to set overnight so make sure to start this tart the day before you plan on serving it.

EQUIPMENT · You will need a stand mixer fitted with a whisk attachment and one piping bag fitted with a medium round tip (#803 or #804).

INGREDIENT NOTES · For the feuilletine base we use Valrhona 66% Caraïbe callets. For the spiced whipped ganache we use Valrhona 35% Ivoire callets. For the maple bourbon ganache we use Valrhona 40% Jivara callets.

INGREDIENTS

1	fully baked chocolate tart shell (*pages 184–187*)

FEUILLETINE BASE

75 g (½ cup)	dark chocolate
38 g (⅓ cup + 1 Tbsp)	feuilletine

SPICED WHIPPED GANACHE

43 g (¼ cup)	white chocolate
74 g (⅓ cup)	whipping cream
½ tsp	vanilla extract or paste
pinch	ground ginger
pinch	ground cinnamon
2 Tbsp	whipping cream, cold

TO MAKE THE FEUILLETINE BASE

1. Slowly melt the dark chocolate over a double boiler or in a microwave on half power. Once the chocolate is fully melted, mix in the feuilletine (*Photos A–B*).

2. Using an offset spatula, gently press the mixture into the bottom of the tart shell, making sure to fill all the corners (*Photo C*). Set aside.

TO MAKE THE SPICED WHIPPED GANACHE

3. Slowly melt the white chocolate over a double boiler or in a microwave on half power.

4. While the chocolate is melting, heat the 74 g (⅓ cup) measure of cream, vanilla, ginger, and cinnamon in a saucepan until just scalding.

5. Pour the hot cream over the white chocolate in three parts, using a spatula to mix well between each addition.

6. Add the 2 Tbsp cold cream and mix until well incorporated. Refrigerate overnight.

CONTINUED

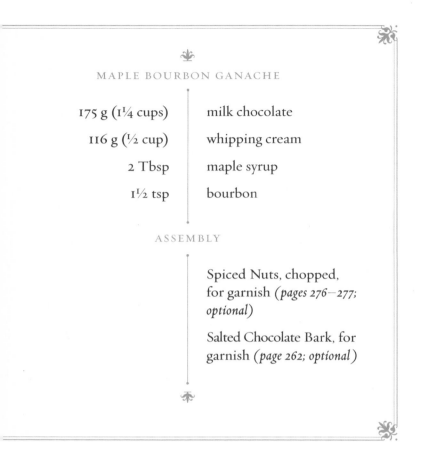

MAPLE BOURBON GANACHE

175 g (1¼ cups)	milk chocolate
116 g (½ cup)	whipping cream
2 Tbsp	maple syrup
1½ tsp	bourbon

ASSEMBLY

Spiced Nuts, chopped, for garnish *(pages 276–277; optional)*

Salted Chocolate Bark, for garnish *(page 262; optional)*

TO MAKE THE MAPLE BOURBON GANACHE ·

7. Slowly melt the milk chocolate over a double boiler or in a microwave on half power.

8. While the chocolate is melting, heat the cream, maple syrup, and bourbon in a saucepan until just scalding.

9. Pour the hot cream over the chocolate in three parts, using a spatula to mix well between each addition.

10. Pour the ganache into the tart shell, making sure not to overfill it (there may be a bit left over). Refrigerate for at least 3 hours, until well set.

TO ASSEMBLE THE TART

11. Place the spiced whipped ganache in a stand mixer bowl and, using the whisk attachment, whip on low speed until the ganache is thickened and shiny and forms soft peaks. Be careful not to overwhip, as the ganache may become grainy.

12. Using a piping bag fitted with a plain round tip, pipe dots of spiced ganache in various sizes on top of the tart.

13. Sprinkle with spiced nuts and make an arrangement with small pieces of salted chocolate bark. Serve at room temperature.

STORAGE · This tart will keep in the refrigerator for up to three days.

Cakes

THE DUKE

MAKES 1 / 8-INCH CAKE

CHOCOLATE CAKE

120 g (½ cup)	hot brewed coffee
30 g (3 Tbsp)	dark chocolate
200 g (1 cup)	sugar
118 g (¾ cup)	all-purpose flour
60 g (½ cup)	cocoa powder
¾ tsp	baking soda
¼ tsp	baking powder
¼ tsp	salt
1	large egg
60 g (¼ cup)	vegetable oil
120 g (½ cup)	buttermilk
½ tsp	vanilla extract or paste

With its winning combination of luscious chocolate cake, velvety frosting, and a layer of salted caramel delightfully tucked away inside, this is by far our most popular cake. For chocolate lovers far and wide, it's become a favourite for birthdays, office parties, and other events.

EQUIPMENT · You will need a round 8-inch cake pan and a stand mixer fitted with a paddle attachment. Also, it's useful to have a cake-decorating turntable for frosting the cake, though not essential.

INGREDIENT NOTES · We use Valrhona 66% Caraïbe callets throughout the recipe and Valrhona cocoa powder in the cake.

TO MAKE THE CHOCOLATE CAKE · Preheat your oven to 325°F (160°C). Line the cake pan with parchment paper and spray it with vegetable oil.

1. In a large bowl, pour the hot coffee over the chocolate a bit at a time, whisking continuously until all the coffee is poured in and the chocolate has completely melted. Set aside.

2. Sift all the dry ingredients together and set aside.

3. Whisk the egg, oil, buttermilk, and vanilla together in a bowl. Slowly whisk the mixture into the melted chocolate and coffee.

4. Add the sifted dry ingredients and whisk until the batter comes together. The batter will appear a bit lumpy. Do not overmix.

5. Pour the batter into the prepared cake pan. Bake for about 45 minutes, or until a toothpick inserted in the centre comes out clean.

6. Allow to cool completely. Gently run a knife around the edge of the pan and flip the cake out. Set aside until you're ready for assembly.

CONTINUED

ASSEMBLY

½ batch	Salted Caramel (*page 273*)

DUKE FROSTING

188 g (1¼ cups)	dark chocolate
½ tsp	fleur de sel or salt
150 g (⅔ cup)	whipping cream
2 Tbsp	water
84 g (⅓ cup + 1 Tbsp)	sugar
1 Tbsp	light corn syrup or glucose
188 g (¾ cup + 1 Tbsp)	unsalted butter, cubed, at room temperature

GLAÇAGE

140 g (1 cup)	dark chocolate
190 g (¾ cup + 1 Tbsp)	whipping cream
2 Tbsp	water
60 g (3 Tbsp)	glucose or light corn syrup

TO MAKE THE DUKE FROSTING

7. Slowly melt the chocolate over a double boiler or in a microwave. Once the chocolate is fully melted, mix in the fleur de sel. Set aside.

8. Heat the whipping cream in the microwave or on the stovetop until scalding. Set aside and try to keep hot while you proceed to the next step.

9. Place the water, sugar, and corn syrup in a small saucepan over medium heat and cook until the sugar turns a dark honey or amber colour (*Photo A*). Do not stir (*see 'Making a Caramel,' pages 271–272*).

10. Once the sugar has reached the right colour, remove from heat and slowly pour in the hot cream (*Photo B*). Stir until well combined (*Photos C–D*). Pour the mixture over the chocolate and fleur de sel in three parts, mixing with a heatproof spatula between additions until smooth (*Photos E–G*). You now have chocolate ganache.

11. Transfer the ganache to a stand mixer bowl and allow to cool to room temperature. Ensure that both the ganache and butter cubes are at room temperature before moving to the next step.

12. With the mixer on low speed, add the butter cubes to the ganache a few at a time, incorporating well between each addition (*Photo H*). Once all the butter has been incorporated, turn the mixer up to medium and beat until the frosting is light and fluffy (*Photo I*).

CONTINUED →

TO ASSEMBLE THE CAKE

13. Using a sharp serrated knife, cut the cake in half horizontally into two layers (*Photo J*). Flip the top layer so that its cut side is facing up.

14. If the salted caramel has been in the refrigerator, warm it in a microwave for a few seconds to soften it slightly—just enough to be easy to spread, but not to the point of being runny. Spread about ½ cup salted caramel over the bottom layer of the cake, leaving about ½ inch around the edge (*Photo K*).

15. Spread about 1 cup of the frosting over the caramel, leaving a bit of space around the edges. Place the other cake layer on top, cut side up so that your cake will have a flat top, and gently press down (*Photos L–M*). If any frosting comes out of the sides, smooth it out with an offset spatula.

16. Transfer the cake to a turntable and spoon about 2 cups of frosting on top, reserving extra frosting to finish the cake. Spread it evenly over the top and sides of the cake and smooth it out with an offset spatula. The smoother you can get the frosting, the more pleasing the end product will be (*Photo N–P*).

17. In preparation for adding the glaçage, using a long offset spatula, gently transfer the cake to a flat plate or pan lined with parchment paper and freeze it for at least 2 hours (or up to a week, if making ahead). You may wish to skip the glaçage and finish the cake now; in that case, transfer the cake to a serving plate or cake stand and skip to step 22.

TO MAKE THE GLAÇAGE · Prepare the glaçage only when ready to finish the cake.

18. Slowly melt the dark chocolate over a double boiler or in a microwave.

19. In a saucepan, heat the whipping cream, water, and glucose until just scalding. Pour the hot cream over the dark chocolate in three parts, mixing with a spatula between additions until smooth.

TO FINISH THE CAKE

20. Remove the cake from the freezer and place it on a flat cooling rack. Position a pan or piece of foil underneath to catch chocolate drippings (*Photo Q*).

21. Using a ladle or measuring cup, pour the glaçage over the top of the cake. Using an offset spatula or the bottom of the ladle, spread the glaçage over the sides, making sure to cover the whole cake. Immediately move the cake to a serving plate or cake stand using a long offset spatula (*Photos R–T*).

22. Decorate the cake with the reserved frosting. We pipe five dots on top and a decorative border around the bottom edge of the cake (*Photo U*).

STORAGE · The Duke will keep at room temperature for up to four days.

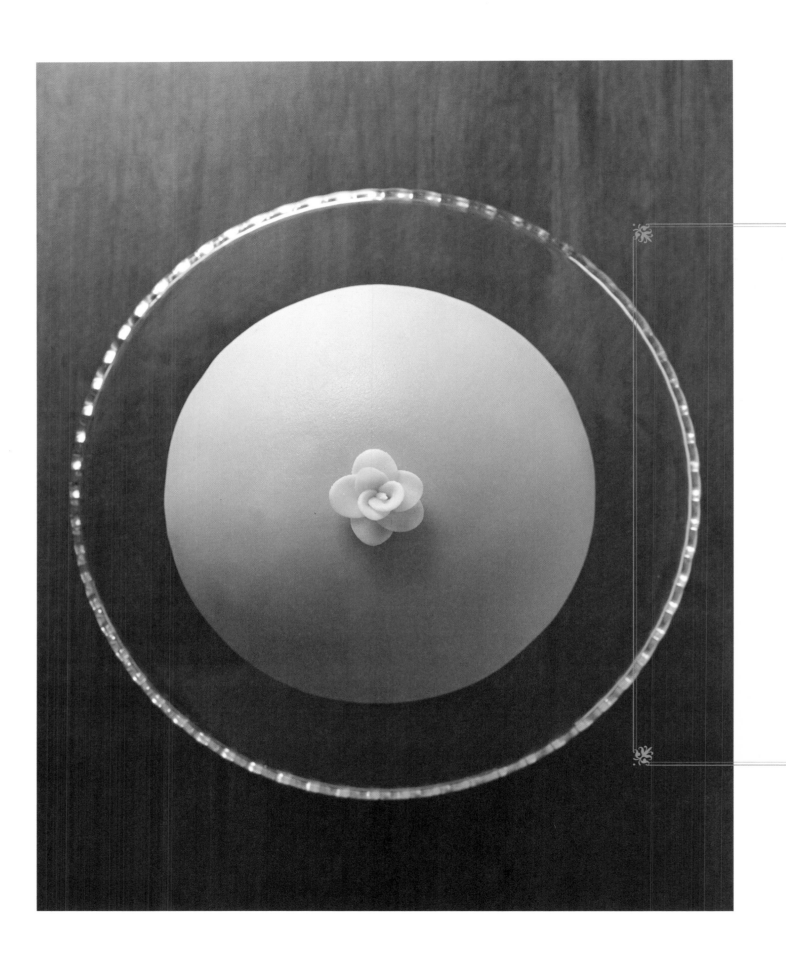

the
DUCHESS

CHIFFON CAKE

85 g (¾ cup)	cake flour
63 g (⅓ cup)	sugar
½ tsp	baking powder
¼ tsp	salt
2 Tbsp	vegetable oil
2	large eggs, separated
3 Tbsp	water
½ tsp	vanilla extract or paste
1 Tbsp	fresh lemon zest
1 Tbsp	sugar
¼ tsp	cream of tartar

SIMPLE SYRUP

50 g (¼ cup)	sugar
62 g (¼ cup)	water

Although my grandmother passed away the year before we opened Duchess, I always thought that she would have loved this, our signature cake. It's based on the prinsesstårta, a traditional Swedish cake that I have a great admiration for. Its contrasting layers and sophisticated marzipan covering make it the perfect choice for us to feature at Duchess. Raspberry and marzipan are a match made in heaven, but if the inspiration strikes, do experiment with other jam flavours and play with the colour of the marzipan. This recipe, with its many steps, will appeal to more adventurous bakers who really want to make a splash at a special event.

EQUIPMENT · You will need a stand mixer fitted with a whisk attachment, an 8-inch round cake pan, a cake turntable, an offset spatula, and ribbon of your choice (½ inch in width).

INGREDIENT NOTES · We use natural, plant-based food colourings. Marzipan is available in specialty food stores and isn't to be confused with almond paste.

TO MAKE THE CHIFFON CAKE · Preheat your oven to 325°F (160°C). Line the bottom of the cake pan with parchment paper, but do not butter or spray it as that will affect the rise of the cake.

1. Sift together the flour, the 63 g (⅓ cup) measure of sugar, the baking powder, and the salt. Set aside.

2. In a bowl, whisk together the oil, egg yolks, water, vanilla, and lemon zest. Add the sifted dry ingredients and whisk until there are no lumps. Set aside.

3. Using a stand mixer, whip the egg whites on medium-high speed until soft peaks form. Gradually add the remaining 1 Tbsp measure of sugar and the cream of tartar. Continue to whip until stiff peaks form.

4. Using a spatula, gently fold the egg whites into the batter until the whites have just disappeared and the batter looks airy and thick. Pour the batter into the lined cake pan.

CONTINUED

MARZIPAN

350 g	marzipan
2 drops	yellow liquid food colouring
4 drops	green liquid food colouring
about 2 Tbsp	icing sugar

ASSEMBLY

⅓ cup	homemade or good-quality store-bought raspberry jam
1 batch	Pastry Cream, chilled *(pages 188–189, steps 1 to 7)*

FINISHING

385 g (1½ cups)	whipping cream
2 Tbsp	icing sugar, plus more for rolling out the marzipan
1 tsp	vanilla extract or paste

5. Bake for 30 to 35 minutes, until the centre springs back to the touch or a toothpick comes out clean. Let the cake cool completely before removing it from the pan.

TO MAKE THE SIMPLE SYRUP AND ASSEMBLE THE CAKE

6. To make simple syrup, place the sugar and water in a small saucepan. Heat until the syrup just comes to a boil. Remove from heat and set aside to cool.

7. Using a sharp serrated knife, cut the cake in half horizontally into two layers.

8. Brush the insides of both cake halves generously with the cooled simple syrup *(Photo A)*.

9. Spread the raspberry jam over the bottom half of the cake, leaving a bit of space around the edge for the jam to expand into when the layers are stacked *(Photo B)*.

10. Top the jam with the pastry cream, again leaving room around the edge. Place the other half of the cake firmly on top, cut side down, and gently press down *(Photos C–D)*.

11. Gently move the cake to a flat plate or pan and freeze it for at least 2 hours (or wrap it and freeze it for up to a week, if you are making the cake ahead).

12. In a small bowl, place 1 Tbsp of the marzipan. Add the yellow food colouring and, using your hands (wear disposable gloves if you have them), work it into the marzipan until it's uniformly yellow. Feel free to add a couple more drops of food colouring if you want to brighten up the colour. If the marzipan feels too wet, work in 1 tsp icing sugar. Wrap and set aside in the refrigerator.

13. Place the remaining marzipan in a bowl and add the green food colouring. As before, work it into the marzipan until it's uniformly green. If the marzipan feels wet, work in 1 to 2 Tbsp icing sugar. Shape the marzipan into a flat circular disk, wrap, and set aside in the refrigerator.

TO FINISH THE CAKE

14. Remove the cake from the freezer and transfer it to a cake turntable. Remove the marzipan from the refrigerator and set it aside.

15. Place the whipping cream, icing sugar, and vanilla in a stand mixer bowl. Using the whisk attachment, whip on medium-high speed until stiff peaks form.

16. Using a sharp serrated knife, trim the sides of the upper cake layer at an angle to form a rounded edge (*Photo E*). If the cake is still too frozen to cut, leave it at room temperature for another 15 minutes, then try again.

17. Place a heaping amount of whipped cream on top of the cake. Using an offset spatula, spread it to completely cover the sides while leaving a heaping dome on top (*Photos F–G*).

18. Starting with your offset spatula held flat at the top of the whipped cream, gently turn the turntable while shaping a dome with the knife until you reach the bottom of the cake (*Photo H*).

19. Refrigerate the cake (still on the turntable) while you prepare the marzipan.

CONTINUED

E *F* *G* *H*

20. Lightly sprinkle a piece of parchment paper with icing sugar and roll out the yellow marzipan on the parchment to about ½ cm thick. Using a circle cutter about 1 cm in diameter (we use the top of a piping tip), cut out 8 circles. Gently roll out the top of each circle to form a petal shape. Form a stem with the leftover yellow marzipan and gently attach each petal to make a rose (*Photos I–L*). Set aside.

21. Sprinkle your work surface with a generous amount of icing sugar. Roll out the green marzipan until you have a circle that is about 10 inches in diameter. The marzipan will likely be sticky so don't be shy with the icing sugar and flip and rotate the dough frequently as you roll it (*Photo M*).

22. Remove the cake from the refrigerator. Centre the green marzipan disk on top of the cake. Using your hands, gently smooth out the marzipan, working your way around the cake from top to bottom. Trim the bottom edge with a sharp knife or a wheel cutter (*Photos N–R*).

23. Using a long offset spatula, gently transfer the cake to a serving plate or cake stand. Using a toothpick, make a small hole in the top of the cake. Insert the rose. Gently line the bottom edge of the cake with the ribbon and secure the ends together with a piece of double-sided tape (*Photos S–T*).

24. Leave the cake out for an hour or so before serving to give it the chance to thaw to room temperature. Once thawed, it can be left out for up to two more hours before serving; otherwise, chill until ready to serve.

STORAGE · The Duchess is best eaten the day it's made. It will keep for up to three days in the refrigerator, but be aware that the marzipan will progressively soften.

LEMON
meringue CAKE

This is our take on the popular lemon meringue cake. Our lemon cream and our salted caramel are a perfect match for the light and fluffy chiffon cake, and the playful meringue exterior is sure to please adults and children alike. Each day at Duchess we carefully caramelize the meringue on these cakes. We are picky about what goes out to the pastry case and even the slightest nick in the browned meringue will disqualify a finished cake. Needless to say, our staff members often get to enjoy this cake as an afternoon snack!

LEMON CREAM

112 g (½ cup + 1 Tbsp)	sugar
63 g (¼ cup)	fresh lemon zest
2	large eggs
85 g (⅓ cup)	fresh lemon juice
150 g (⅔ cup)	unsalted butter, cubed

CHIFFON CAKE

85 g (¾ cup)	cake flour
63 g (⅓ cup)	sugar
½ tsp	baking powder
¼ tsp	salt
2 Tbsp	vegetable oil
2	large eggs, separated
3 Tbsp	water
½ tsp	vanilla extract or paste
1 Tbsp	fresh lemon zest
1 Tbsp	sugar
¼ tsp	cream of tartar

EQUIPMENT · You will need a stand mixer with the whisk and paddle attachments, an 8-inch round cake pan, an instant-read digital thermometer, an offset spatula, and a culinary torch. A cake turntable will help with torching the meringue evenly but isn't essential.

TO MAKE THE LEMON CREAM

1. In a bowl, rub the lemon zest into the sugar using your fingers. This will help bring the oils out of the zest. Add the eggs and whisk until combined. Add the lemon juice and whisk again.

2. Transfer to a double boiler. Cook for 30 to 45 minutes, whisking and scraping down the sides every 5 to 10 minutes, until the mixture is thick and has darkened significantly in colour.

3. As soon as the lemon mixture has finished cooking, strain out the zest through a fine mesh strainer. Use the back of a spatula or a wooden spoon to try and get as much cream through the strainer as you can—you don't want to lose any of that great lemon flavour!

4. Gradually whisk the butter cubes into the strained lemon cream until the mixture is completely smooth and all the butter is incorporated. Or, use an immersion blender to blend in the butter; this will eliminate any graininess and leave you with velvety, extra-smooth lemon cream.

5. Cover the lemon cream and refrigerate for 3 to 4 hours, until set.

CONTINUED

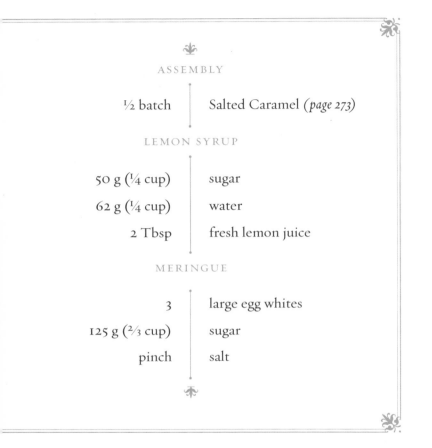

ASSEMBLY

½ batch	Salted Caramel (*page 273*)

LEMON SYRUP

50 g (¼ cup)	sugar
62 g (¼ cup)	water
2 Tbsp	fresh lemon juice

MERINGUE

3	large egg whites
125 g (⅔ cup)	sugar
pinch	salt

TO MAKE THE CHIFFON CAKE · Preheat your oven to 325°F (160°C). Line the bottom of the cake pan with parchment paper, but do not butter or spray it as that will affect the rise of the cake.

6. Sift together the flour, the 63 g (⅓ cup) measure of sugar, the baking powder, and the salt. Set aside.

7. In a bowl, whisk together the oil, egg yolks, water, vanilla, and lemon zest. Add the sifted dry ingredients and whisk until there are no lumps. Set aside.

8. Fit your stand mixer with the whisk attachment and whip the egg whites on medium-high speed until soft peaks form. Gradually add the 1 Tbsp measure of sugar and the cream of tartar. Continue to whip until stiff peaks form.

9. Using a spatula, gently fold the egg whites into the batter until the whites have just disappeared and the batter looks airy and thick. Pour the batter into the cake pan.

10. Bake for 30 to 35 minutes, until the centre springs back to the touch or a toothpick comes out clean. Let the cake cool completely before removing it from the pan.

A *B* *C* *D*

11. To make the lemon syrup, place the sugar, water, and lemon juice in a small saucepan. Heat until the syrup just comes to a boil. Remove from heat and set aside to cool.

12. Using a sharp serrated knife, cut the cake in half horizontally into two layers.

13. Brush the insides of both cake halves generously with the cooled lemon syrup (*Photo A*).

14. If the salted caramel has been in the refrigerator, warm it in a microwave for a few seconds to soften it slightly—just enough to be easy to spread, but not to the point of being runny. Spread about ½ cup of caramel over the bottom half of the cake, leaving a bit of space around the edge for it to expand into when the layers are stacked (*Photo B*).

15. Top the salted caramel with the lemon cream, again leaving space around the edge of the cake. Place the other half of the cake on top, cut side down, and gently press down (*Photos C–D*).

16. Gently move the cake to a flat plate or pan and freeze it for 30 minutes (or wrap it and freeze it for up to a week, if you are making the cake ahead).

TO FINISH THE CAKE

17. Prepare the meringue just before frosting the cake. Heat the egg whites, sugar, and salt in a stand mixer bowl fitted over a double boiler, whisking often, until the mixture reaches 130°F (55°C). Remove from heat and, using your stand mixer fitted with the whisk attachment, whip on high until the meringue is shiny and stiff peaks form.

18. Place the frozen cake on a cake-decorating turntable. Heap the meringue on the top of the cake and spread it with an offset spatula to cover the whole cake. Be sure not to spend too long on this step as the meringue will start to fall and lose its structure (*Photos E–G*).

19. Using a culinary torch, starting at the bottom of the cake, turn the turntable slowly as you caramelize the meringue. Try to keep a steady hand as you move the torch slowly over the whole cake at a distance of 1 to 2 inches (*Photo H*).

20. Using a large offset spatula or a flat cake server, transfer the cake to a plate or cake stand for cutting and serving.

STORAGE · This cake will keep in the refrigerator for up to four days. Do not freeze once finished with meringue.

E   F   G   H

Pâte à Choux

PÂTE À CHOUX · The light and airy pâte à choux, or choux pastry, provides the foundation for many delicious pastries such as éclairs and chouquettes (cream puffs). If done right, the dough will puff up and form a hollow centre that can be filled with anything you like. In French pastries this is often pastry cream or fresh fruit. Although pâte à choux usually features sweet fillings, the dough itself has almost no sugar, so you can easily fill it with something savoury like cream cheese and smoked salmon.

At Duchess, we feature a different éclair flavour every month, which gives our pastry chefs opportunities to experiment and get creative. In this chapter we've featured a few of our favourites as well as recipes for the more elaborate St. Honoré and Paris–Brest. You can also use pâte à choux to make chouquettes and fill them with any of the éclair fillings or whatever else tickles your fancy. •

PÂTE À CHOUX

INGREDIENTS

95 g (¼ cup + 2 Tbsp)	skim milk
95 g (¼ cup + 2 Tbsp)	water
87 g (¼ cup + 2 Tbsp)	unsalted butter
½ tsp	salt
½ tsp	sugar
105 g (⅔ cup)	all-purpose flour
3	large eggs

FOR CHOUQUETTES & ÉCLAIRS

1	large egg yolk
2 tsp	whipping cream or whole milk

FOR PARIS—BRESTS

	sliced almonds

EQUIPMENT · You will need a stand mixer fitted with a paddle attachment, a baking sheet, and a piping bag fitted with the appropriate piping tip for your desired dough shape (see page 230). Before you make your dough, make sure to prepare a template for piping the dough according to your desired shape (see page 230).

TO MAKE THE PÂTE À CHOUX · Preheat the oven to 375°F (190°C). Line the baking sheet with parchment paper.

1. Place the skim milk, water, butter, salt, and sugar in a saucepan and bring to a simmer.

2. Turn the heat down to low, add the flour all at once, and begin stirring with a flat wooden spoon (Photo A). The dough will form a mass and start pulling away from the sides of the pan (Photo B). Stir vigorously without stopping for 4 to 5 minutes. The dough will darken a bit in colour and slightly dry out (Photo C), which is what you want, as otherwise it may be too runny to pipe.

3. Immediately transfer the dough into a stand mixer bowl. With the mixer on medium-low speed, add the eggs one at time, mixing well between each addition. Your pâte à choux is now ready to pipe (Photo D).

4. Preheat your oven to 375°F (190°C) and immediately pipe the dough according to the specific instructions for your desired shape on page 230.

TO BAKE THE PÂTE À CHOUX · As soon as it's piped, bake the pâte à choux for 30 minutes. Do not open the oven door during baking. After 30 minutes, prop the oven door open with a wooden spoon to let the built-up steam escape and slightly dry out the choux. Bake for another 5 minutes with the door still propped open, or until you can feel that the outside of the dough has crisped up.

STORAGE · Once baked, choux pastries should be filled and served over the next two days. If you didn't fill them right away and they have gone soft, re-crisp in the oven for 4 to 6 minutes at 350°F (180°C). They can also be frozen for up to two months: in that case, place them frozen in a 350°F (180°C) oven until warmed through and crispy (6 to 8 minutes). Allow to cool before filling.

TIPS & TRICKS · Here are a few simple tips for making the perfect pâte à choux:

— Even though it's quite tiring, stir the dough without stopping for the full 4 to 5 minutes while it's cooking. The dough needs to dry out as it cooks, and the most common mistake people make is not stirring it for long enough. If you undercook it, your pâte à choux will come out flat after baking and won't have enough of a hollow centre for you to fill.

— Pipe the pâte à choux immediately after making it.

— Do not open the oven door during the first 30 minutes of baking as this will release the steam and cause the pastry to flatten.

— If after 35 minutes in the oven your pâte à choux doesn't feel crispy, it's fine to leave it in the oven for another 4 to 5 minutes.

— It really helps to fill the pâte à choux as close to serving time as possible. The longer they sit filled, the softer the texture of the pastry will become. We like our pâte à choux to be slightly crisp when we bite into it.

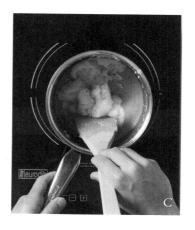

How to pipe PÂTE À CHOUX

ÉCLAIRS · Make a template by drawing 2 sets of 2 parallel lines along the length of your parchment paper about 5 inches apart. Flip the template over so the lines are face down and using a small amount of the pâte à choux, glue down the corners of the template to the baking sheet. This will prevent the parchment from slipping around while you're piping your dough.

1. Fit a piping bag with a large round tip (#809). Fill the bag with the pâte à choux.

2. Using the template as a guide, starting about 2 inches from the edge of the parchment paper, pipe dough in straight lines 5 inches long, letting the dough fall slowly from the tip as you pipe (*Photo A*).

3. In a small bowl, whisk together the egg yolk and whipping cream for the egg wash. Use a fork to run the egg wash over the top of each éclair (*Photo B*).

4. Bake immediately (*see 'To Bake the Pâte à Choux,' page 229*).

PARIS—BRESTS · Make a template by drawing 5 × 3-inch circles onto your parchment paper spaced about 2 inches apart (we trace around a glass). Flip the template over so the lines are face down and using a small amount of the pâte à choux, glue down the corners of the template to the baking sheet. This will prevent the parchment from slipping around while you're piping your dough.

1. Fit a piping bag with a large open star tip (#828 or #829). Fill the bag with the pâte à choux.

2. Using the template as a guide, pipe dough around the circles to form rings (*Photo C*).

3. Sprinkle sliced almonds onto the rings (*Photo D*) and gently tap the baking sheet to shake away any excess.

4. Bake immediately (*see 'To Bake the Pâte à Choux,' page 229*).

CHOUQUETTES & ST. HONORÉ · Make a template by drawing either 14 × 1-inch circles (for chouquettes) or 7 × 2-inch circles (for a St. Honoré) onto your parchment paper spaced about 2 inches apart (we trace around a glass). Flip the template over so the lines are face down and using a small amount of the pâte à choux, glue down the corners of the template to the baking sheet. This will prevent the parchment from slipping around while you're piping your dough.

1. Fit a piping bag with a medium round tip (#804). Fill the bag with the pâte à choux.

2. Using the template as a guide, hold the piping bag vertically with the tip ½ inch above the tray and pipe circles onto the parchment (*Photo E*). Try to keep the bag steady so that the dough falls continuously into the centre of the circle.

3. In a small bowl, whisk together the egg yolk and whipping cream for the egg wash. Use your finger to gently run egg wash over the top of each circle, making sure to smooth down any bumps (*Photo F*).

4. Bake immediately (*see 'To Bake the Pâte à Choux,' page 229*).

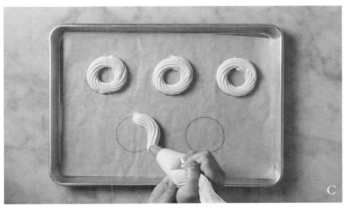

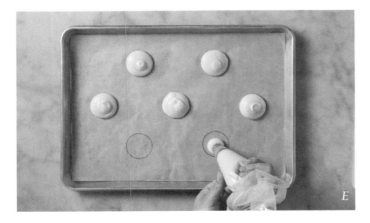

CLASSIC ÉCLAIRS

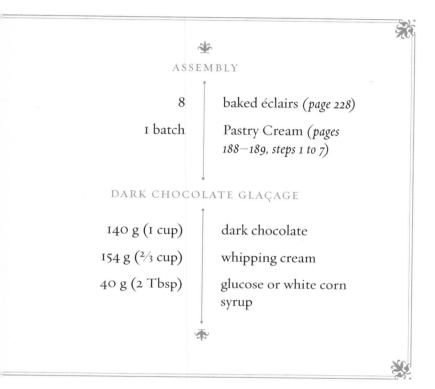

ASSEMBLY

8	baked éclairs (*page 228*)
1 batch	Pastry Cream (*pages 188—189, steps 1 to 7*)

DARK CHOCOLATE GLAÇAGE

140 g (1 cup)	dark chocolate
154 g (⅔ cup)	whipping cream
40 g (2 Tbsp)	glucose or white corn syrup

Nothing beats a classic éclair, with its elegantly shaped pastry and glossy chocolate finish concealing an irresistible burst of pastry cream. When this pastry originated in France in the nine-teenth century it was known as 'pain à la duchesse,' but it soon came to be called 'éclair,' which means lightning. I certainly find it difficult to eat one slowly! Although at Duchess we like to get creative with our monthly éclair flavours, our classic éclair, in its perfect simplicity, is always a favourite.

Chouquettes, or cream puffs, are exactly the same as éclairs apart from their shape. To make chouquettes, simply pipe the dough in 1-inch circles instead of in 5-inch lengths.

EQUIPMENT · You will need a piping bag.

INGREDIENT NOTE · For the dark chocolate we use Valrhona 66% Caraïbe callets.

TO MAKE THE DARK CHOCOLATE GLAÇAGE

1. Slowly melt the chocolate over a double boiler or in a microwave on half power. In a saucepan, heat the whipping cream and glucose until just scalding.

2. Pour the hot cream over the melted chocolate in three parts, mixing with a spatula between addi-tions until smooth. If not using right away, refriger-ate and, when ready to dip your éclairs, reheat to the proper consistency as described in step 5.

CONTINUED

TO ASSEMBLE THE ÉCLAIRS

3. Turn the éclairs over so that the flat sides are facing up. Using a small round piping tip or the tip of a paring knife, poke a small hole near each end of each éclair *(Photo A)*.

4. Using a spatula or wooden spoon, loosen the pastry cream to make it easier to pipe. Fill a piping bag with the pastry cream and cut a small hole off the end of the bag. For each éclair, insert the tip of the piping bag into one of the holes and fill about halfway. Repeat with the second hole, until filling starts to come out the other end *(Photo B)*.

5. Test your glaçage to make sure it's at the right consistency. You want it to be slightly warm and feel a bit thick when you stir it. If it's too warm it will slide off the éclair after you dip it and if it's too cool it will be too thick to dip. If necessary, warm it in the microwave in 10-second intervals or chill for a few minutes to cool it down.

6. Pick up an éclair by the sides and dip it top down into the glaçage. Hold it vertically to let any excess chocolate drip off the bottom *(Photo C)*. Use your finger to wipe away the drips.

7. Once all the éclairs have been dipped, refrigerate for at least 15 minutes to allow the glaçage to set.

STORAGE · Éclairs are best eaten within six hours of assembly. They will keep for up to two days in the refrigerator, though the pastry will go a bit soft.

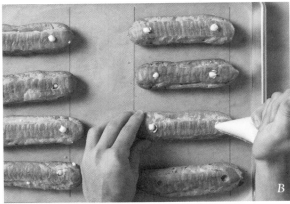

RASPBERRY
dark chocolate
ÉCLAIRS

EQUIPMENT · You will need an instant-read digital thermometer, a fine mesh strainer, and two piping bags, one fitted with a medium round piping tip (#803 or #804).

INGREDIENT NOTE · For the dark chocolate we use Valrhona 66% Caraïbe callets.

TO MAKE THE RASPBERRY CURD FILLING

1. Place the raspberry purée, sugar, and eggs over a double boiler and whisk well. Cook over medium heat, whisking constantly, until the curd reaches 82°C (180°F). The mixture will have started to thicken. Remove from heat and, using a fine mesh strainer, strain into a bowl.

2. Add the butter to the hot curd mixture and whisk until smooth. Refrigerate the curd for at least 1 hour, until set.

TO MAKE THE DARK CHOCOLATE GANACHE

3. Slowly melt the chocolate over a double boiler or in a microwave on half power. In a saucepan, heat the whipping cream and glucose until just scalding.

4. Pour the hot cream over the melted chocolate in three parts, mixing with a spatula between additions until smooth. Refrigerate for 2 hours, or until set.

CONTINUED

ASSEMBLY

| 8 | baked éclairs (*page 228*) |
| | fresh raspberries, for finishing |

RASPBERRY CURD FILLING

130 g (½ cup)	raspberry purée (*see 'Fruit Purées,' page 19*)
50 g (¼ cup)	sugar
2	large eggs
130 g (½ cup + 1 Tbsp)	unsalted butter, cold

DARK CHOCOLATE GANACHE

70 g (½ cup)	dark chocolate
77 g (⅓ cup)	whipping cream
20 g (1 Tbsp)	glucose or white corn syrup

5. Remove the ganache from the refrigerator to allow it to come to room temperature while you fill the éclairs.

6. Using a small, sharp serrated knife, cut the tops off the éclairs, leaving an edge (*Photo A*). Discard the tops.

7. Remove the raspberry curd from the refrigerator and loosen it with a spatula or wooden spoon. Fill one of the piping bags with the curd and cut off the tip to leave a hole about 2 cm in diameter.

8. Fill each éclair with curd, making sure to get in the corners. Gently press fresh raspberries (whole or halved) into the piped curd, leaving space in between to pipe chocolate ganache (*Photo B*).

9. Fill the tipped piping bag with the ganache. Pipe large dots of ganache between the raspberries (*Photo C*).

STORAGE · Éclairs are best eaten within six hours of assembly. They will keep for up to two days in the refrigerator, though the pastry will go a bit soft.

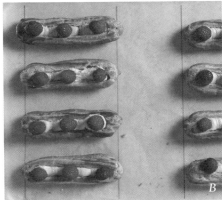

RHUBARB
crumb éclairs

EQUIPMENT · You will need a small baking sheet,
a stand or hand mixer fitted with a whisk attachment,
and a piping bag.

INGREDIENT NOTE · For the white chocolate in the
spiced glaze, we use Valrhona 35% Ivoire callets.

ASSEMBLY

8	baked éclairs (*page 228*)

RHUBARB FILLING

165 g (1½ cups)	rhubarb, cut into ½-inch pieces
½ tsp	ground ginger
75 g (¼ cup + 2 Tbsp)	sugar
1½ tsp	lemon juice
175 g (¾ cup)	whipping cream
2 Tbsp	icing sugar

TO MAKE THE RHUBARB FILLING

1. In a saucepan over medium-low heat, place the rhubarb, ginger, sugar, and lemon juice. Cook until the rhubarb is soft and has broken down. Remove from heat and set aside to cool.

2. Using a stand mixer or a hand mixer, whip the whipping cream and the icing sugar until stiff peaks form.

3. Once your rhubarb is at room temperature, use a fork to break it up as much as you can.

4. Using a spatula, gently fold the whipped cream into the rhubarb. Refrigerate until ready to use.

TO MAKE THE CRUMB TOPPING

5. In a bowl, combine the oats, flour, sugar, and cinnamon. Using your hands, work the butter into the dry ingredients until large clumps form.

6. Spread the crumb on the lined baking sheet and bake for 10 minutes, or until light golden brown. Set aside to cool.

CONTINUED

CRUMB TOPPING

28 g (¼ cup)	old-fashioned rolled oats
3 Tbsp	all-purpose flour
2 Tbsp	firmly packed golden brown sugar
pinch	ground cinnamon
2 Tbsp	unsalted butter

SPICED GLAZE

62 g (¼ cup)	whipping cream
3 Tbsp	pomegranate or cherry juice
2 Tbsp	glucose or white corn syrup
pinch	ground ginger
pinch	ground nutmeg
1	cinnamon stick
pinch	ground cloves
140 g (1 cup)	white chocolate

TO MAKE THE SPICED GLAZE

7. In a small saucepan over medium heat, combine the cream, pomegranate juice, glucose, and spices. Heat until just scalding. Remove from heat and take out the cinnamon stick.

8. Slowly melt the white chocolate over a double boiler or in a microwave on half power.

9. Pour the hot cream mixture over the melted white chocolate in three parts, mixing with a spatula between additions until smooth.

TO ASSEMBLE THE ÉCLAIRS

10. Turn the éclairs over so that the flat sides are facing up. Using a small round piping tip or the tip of a paring knife, poke a small hole near each end of each éclair.

11. Fill a piping bag with the rhubarb filling and cut a small hole off the end of the bag. For each éclair, insert the tip of the piping bag into one of the holes and fill about halfway. Repeat with the second hole, until filling starts to come out the other end.

12. Test your spiced glaze to make sure it's at the right consistency. You want it to be slightly warm and feel a bit thick when you stir it. If it's too warm it will slide off the éclair after you dip it and if it's too cool it will be too thick to dip. If necessary, warm it in the microwave in 10-second intervals or chill for a few minutes to cool it down.

13. Pick up an éclair by the sides and dip it top down into the glaze. Hold it vertically to let any excess glaze drip off the bottom. Use your finger to wipe away the drips.

14. Once all the éclairs have been dipped, sprinkle the tops with the baked crumb and refrigerate for at least 15 minutes to allow the glaze to set.

STORAGE · Éclairs are best eaten within six hours of assembly. They will keep for up to two days in the refrigerator, though the pastry will go a bit soft.

PARIS—BREST

The Paris—Brest was created in the late 1800s to commemorate a bicycle race between the cities of Paris and Brest—hence the bicycle wheel shape. It features choux pastry, creamy praline mousseline, and crunchy candied hazelnuts. Right from the moment I tasted my first Paris—Brest, I knew that when we opened Duchess we would serve this legendary French pastry.

Although this recipe has several parts, the end result is well worth the effort. The praline mousseline calls for praline paste, available in specialty baking stores. If you can't find it, you can make it yourself or use Nutella. This recipe will make double the required amount of candied hazelnuts. Keep the leftovers for snacking or for topping ice cream. If you wish, you can use plain roasted hazelnuts and skip the candying.

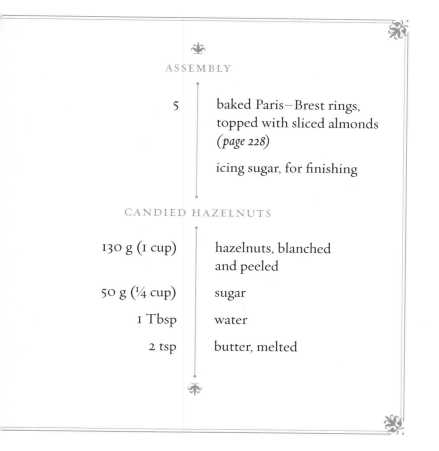

ASSEMBLY

5	baked Paris—Brest rings, topped with sliced almonds (*page 228*)
	icing sugar, for finishing

CANDIED HAZELNUTS

130 g (1 cup)	hazelnuts, blanched and peeled
50 g (¼ cup)	sugar
1 Tbsp	water
2 tsp	butter, melted

EQUIPMENT · You will need a small baking sheet, a stand mixer fitted with a whisk attachment, an instant-read digital thermometer, a piping bag fitted with a large star tip (#829), and a cake turntable (optional).

TO MAKE THE CANDIED HAZELNUTS

1. Heat your oven to 350°F (180°C). Spread out the hazelnuts on a small baking sheet and heat them in the oven until warmed, about 5 minutes. Keep them warm while you cook the sugar.

2. In a small saucepan just large enough to hold the nuts, combine the sugar and water and cook over medium heat until the mixture reaches 117°C (242°F).

3. Make sure the nuts are warm, and then add them to the cooked sugar (if the nuts aren't warm enough the sugar will seize). Stir with a wooden spoon until the sugar has crystallized on the nuts. They will look dry and white.

4. Transfer the nuts to a larger saucepan placed over low heat. Stir constantly until caramelized. If the nuts seem to be caramelizing too quickly, remove from heat briefly while continuing to stir. The nuts are ready when they are shiny and dark caramel in colour.

CONTINUED

PRALINE MOUSSELINE

2	large egg whites
83 g (⅓ cup + 1 Tbsp)	sugar
pinch	salt
226 g (1 cup)	unsalted butter, cubed, at room temperature
140 g (½ cup)	praline paste
116 g (½ cup)	whipping cream

5. Remove from heat and add the butter, stirring until the nuts are coated. Immediately pour the hot nuts onto a baking sheet and separate them with a wooden spoon to prevent them from sticking together. They will be very hot at this point so be careful not to touch them.

6. Once the nuts are cool, you can break up any large chunks with your hands.

TO MAKE THE PRALINE MOUSSELINE

7. Heat the egg whites, sugar, and salt in a stand mixer bowl fitted over a double boiler, whisking often, until the mixture reaches 130°F (55°C). Remove from heat, fit the bowl to your stand mixer fitted with a whisk attachment, and whip on high speed until the meringue is shiny and stiff peaks have formed.

8. Turn the mixer off and change to the paddle attachment. With the mixer on medium speed, add the butter cubes, a few at a time. Mix until light and fluffy.

9. Turn the mixer back down to low. Add the praline paste to the buttercream in two parts, scraping down the sides of the bowl after each addition.

10. In a separate stand mixer bowl, whip the whipping cream until it forms stiff peaks. Using a spatula, fold the whipped cream into the buttercream to finish the praline mousseline. At this point, you can store it in the refrigerator for up to three days or freeze it for up to two weeks.

TO ASSEMBLE THE PARIS–BRESTS

11. Using a serrated bread knife, gently slice the baked choux rings in half horizontally.

12. Make sure that your praline mousseline is stiff enough to pipe. If it's too soft, refrigerate it for 10 to 15 minutes to stiffen it up a little; if it cools down too much, whip it up again in the mixer using a paddle attachment.

13. Fill the piping bag with the praline mousseline. For each Paris–Brest, place the bottom half of a choux ring on a cake turntable or a flat plate. Pipe loops of buttercream while turning the ring *(Photo A)*.

14. Press candied hazelnuts around the outside of the piped mousseline *(Photo B)*. Gently top with the other half of the ring and dust with icing sugar *(Photo C)*.

15. Transfer the finished Paris–Brests to individual serving plates and serve immediately. Or, refrigerate for up to six hours, bringing back to room temperature before serving.

STORAGE · Paris–Brests are best eaten within six hours of assembly. They will keep for up to two days in the refrigerator, though the pastry will go a bit soft.

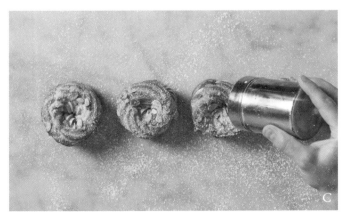

Puff Pastry

Puff pastry dough must rest for at least eight hours before you laminate it, so you'll need to plan for that. Unbaked dough will keep well in the freezer for up to three months, so you might find it convenient to make it in large batches and freeze it in sheets. You will have more success with this recipe if you weigh your ingredients rather than measuring them by volume. For a detailed discussion of laminated doughs, see page 57.

INGREDIENTS

185 g (¾ cup + 1 Tbsp)	unsalted butter (for the butter plaque)
370 g (2¾ cups)	bread flour
112 g (½ cup)	unsalted butter (for the dough)
9 g (2 tsp)	salt
160 g (⅔ cup)	ice water

EQUIPMENT · You will need a stand mixer fitted with a paddle attachment, a resealable plastic bag 7 inches in width, two baking sheets, and a plastic bowl scraper.

INGREDIENT NOTES · Like croissant dough, puff pastry is very sensitive to the fat content of the butter used. If possible use butter with between 82% and 84% butterfat (*see 'A Note on Butter,' page 57*).

TO PREPARE THE DOUGH

1. Remove the butter for the butter plaque from the refrigerator and set aside.

2. Place the flour, butter for the dough, and salt in a stand mixer bowl. With a paddle attachment, mix on medium speed until the texture is sandy (*Photo A*).

3. Turn the mixer down to low and very slowly pour in the ice water (*Photo B*). Mix until well combined.

4. On a lightly floured surface, roll the dough out into a rectangular shape about 7½ by 10½ inches (*Photo C*)—that is, just over double the size of the butter plaque you are going to make in step 5. Line a baking sheet with parchment paper. Transfer the dough to the sheet and cover well with plastic wrap. Refrigerate for at least 8 hours or overnight.

5. Once the dough is in the refrigerator, prepare your butter plaque. Put the set-aside butter into a resealable plastic bag 7 inches wide (*Photo D*). With the bag's zip open to allow air to escape, use a rolling pin to press the butter into the bottom corners of the bag (*Photo E*). Once the butter is well into the corners, continue to roll it until it's 5 inches in length from the bottom of the bag. Use a bench scraper to create a perfect edge at the 5-inch mark (*Photo F*). Seal the bag and refrigerate.

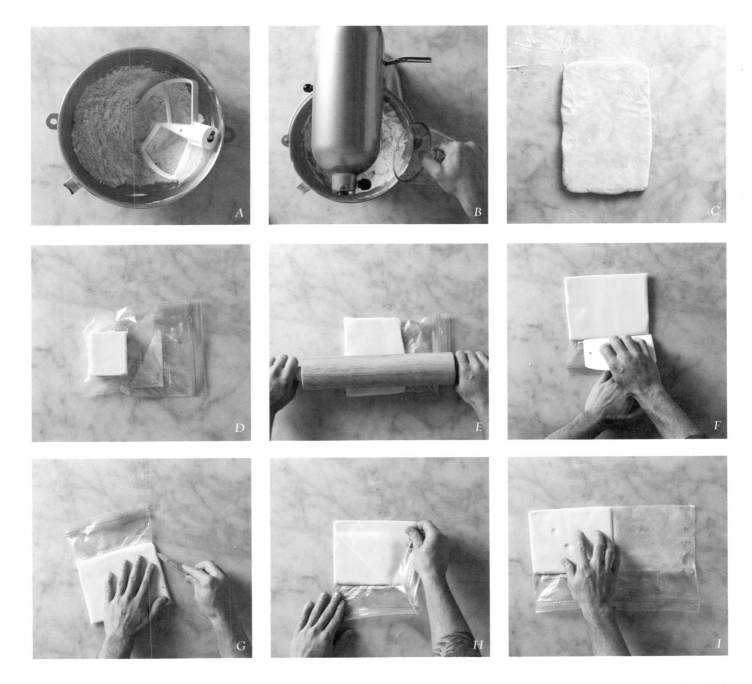

CONTINUED

6. Remove the butter plaque from the refrigerator 20 to 30 minutes before you intend to start rolling your dough. Cut the bag open along the sides, remove the bag's top layer (Photos G–H), and set the butter plaque on the counter to sit at room temperature, keeping it on the bottom half of the bag. The amount of time the butter plaque needs to sit depends on how warm your kitchen is. Getting this right is key to the success of your puff pastry. The idea is to get your butter to the right temperature so that it's pliable enough to roll into the dough without cracking, but not so warm that it leaks out of the sides during rolling. Every 5 minutes, check the butter plaque's texture by pressing into it lightly with your finger. It's ready when it feels like modeling clay and a slight indent forms with little pressure (Photo I). Immediately proceed to step 7 when your butter reaches this point.

7. Remove the dough from the refrigerator, unwrap it, and transfer it to a lightly floured surface. Make sure it measures 7½ by 10½ inches and adjust if necessary.

8. Flip the butter plaque onto one side of the dough and gently peel away the plastic bag (Photo J). Cut the dough in half and flip the cut half over onto the butter plaque, like a sandwich (Photos K–L).

9. Crimp the edges of the dough to hold in the butter plaque and keep the dough together (Photo M). Using a rolling pin, gently press the top of the dough to start joining the dough and the butter together. Flip the dough over and repeat on the other side (Photo N). At this point you should be able to feel whether your butter is pliable enough to move with the dough. If it feels too hard, let it rest at room temperature for another 5 minutes and try again.

10. Roll the dough out to an 8-by-20-inch rectangle (Photo O). Trim off about ½ inch of dough from the short edges.

11. Fold the dough in thirds like you're folding a letter (Photos P–R). This is called a single fold. Wrap the dough, place it on a baking sheet, and return it to the refrigerator for 20 minutes.

12. Repeat steps 10 and 11 four more times, making sure you're rolling out the dough lengthwise with the seam everytime. Once you've completed all five single folds, let the dough rest in the refrigerator for 45 minutes.

13. Roll the puff pastry out to an 11-by-15-inch sheet and place it on a baking sheet lined with parchment paper (Photo S). Return to the refrigerator and chill until cold. At this point you can wrap it and refrigerate it for up to two days or freeze it for up to three months. If you freeze it, let it defrost overnight in the refrigerator before baking.

TO BAKE THE PUFF PASTRY · Preheat your oven to 400°F (205°C).

14. Cover the puff pastry with a sheet of parchment paper and then with a second baking sheet weighed down with an ovenproof dish. This will prevent the pastry from puffing up too much during baking. Make sure the weight is no more than 1.5 kg, otherwise it will crush the layers and prevent the puff pastry from baking properly.

15. Bake for 1 hour and 20 minutes. Remove from the oven and remove the weight, baking sheet, and parchment paper. Immediately sift a layer of icing sugar over the baked pastry (Photo T) and put it back in the oven under a broiler for 2 to 3 minutes, until most of the icing sugar is melted and it looks shiny and caramelized (Photo U). Keep a watchful eye on it as this will happen quickly and you don't want to burn your puff pastry. You now have a baked puff pastry sheet ready to use to make a St. Honoré (see page 249) or Mille-feuilles (see page 253).

STORAGE · The baked puff pastry sheet can be kept at room temperature for up to four days before using it.

DUCHESS
St. Honoré

Named after the patron saint of pastry chefs and bakers, this dessert combines two classic pastries into one: puff pastry and pâte à choux (choux pastry). A layer of puff pastry acts as a base for large chouquettes (cream puffs) dipped in caramel, filled with pastry cream, and topped with fresh whipped cream. We put our own spin on this legendary pastry by incorporating marmalade and Earl Grey tea for the perfect afternoon indulgence.

This dessert is best eaten the day it's assembled, but you can make most of its elements ahead of time and have them ready for assembling the day you plan on serving it. The puff pastry can be made well in advance and kept frozen until needed.

EQUIPMENT · You will need two piping bags, one fitted with a St. Honoré tip (#880) or a star tip of your choice (#826–829), and a stand mixer fitted with a whisk attachment.

EARL GREY PASTRY CREAM

365 g (1½ cups)	whole milk
8 g (2 Tbsp)	Earl Grey tea leaves
80 g (⅓ cup + 1 Tbsp)	sugar
80 g (about 4 large)	egg yolks
23 g (2 Tbsp)	cornstarch
¾ tsp	salt
150 g (⅔ cup)	unsalted butter, cubed

TO MAKE THE EARL GREY PASTRY CREAM

1. In a saucepan over medium-low heat, toast the Earl Grey tea leaves, stirring frequently, until very fragrant. Add the milk and heat to scalding. Remove from heat and allow the tea to steep for 5 minutes.

2. While the tea is steeping, place the sugar and egg yolks in a bowl and whisk until the yolks have lightened in colour. This will take a few minutes of vigorous whisking. Whisk in the cornstarch and salt.

3. Bring the milk back up to scalding and strain to discard the tea. Slowly drizzle the hot milk into the yolk mixture while continuing to whisk. If you add the hot milk too quickly the eggs will curdle and your pastry cream will come out lumpy.

4. Once all the milk has been added, transfer the mixture back to the saucepan and place over medium heat. Whisking constantly, bring the mixture to a boil, and continue cooking for 5 minutes more.

CONTINUED

CARAMEL

200 g (1 cup)	sugar
60 g (¼ cup)	water
80 g (¼ cup)	glucose or white corn syrup

ASSEMBLY

1 × 11-by-15-inch sheet	Puff Pastry, baked and caramelized (*page 244*)
½ cup	homemade or good-quality marmalade
7 or 8	baked 2-inch chouquettes (*page 228*)
242 g (1 cup)	whipping cream
1 Tbsp	icing sugar
1 tsp	vanilla extract or paste

5. Remove from heat. Immediately strain the pastry cream through a fine mesh strainer to remove any lumps. Add the butter and whisk until smooth; or, if you want your pastry cream even smoother, use an immersion blender.

6. Cover the pastry cream and refrigerate for 2 to 3 hours, until set.

TO ASSEMBLE THE ST. HONORÉ

7. Using a plate or circle as a guide, cut an 8-inch circle out of the puff pastry (*Photo A*). Using a small amount of marmalade, glue the puff pastry onto a serving plate or cake stand before assembling it.

8. Spread the marmalade evenly over the puff pastry circle (*Photo B*).

9. Turn the chouquettes over so that the flat sides are facing up. Using a small round piping tip or the tip of a paring knife, poke a small hole in the bottom of each chouquette.

10. Using a spatula or wooden spoon, loosen the chilled Earl Grey pastry cream to make it easier to pipe. Fill a piping bag with the pastry cream and cut a small hole in the end of the bag. For each chouquette, insert the tip of the piping bag into the hole and fill (*Photo C*). Set the chouquettes aside.

11. To make the caramel, place the sugar, water, and glucose in a small saucepan. Cook on medium-low heat until the sugar is light amber in colour. Remove from heat and immediately proceed to the next step.

12. Pick up each chouquette by its sides and dip it top down into the caramel. Let the excess caramel drip off (*Photo D*) and leave to cool (*Photo E*). Be very careful when working with caramel in this way. If it touches your skin it will burn you instantly.

13. Once dipped, arrange the chouquettes in a ring along the edge of the marmalade-covered puff pastry circle (*Photo F*).

14. Pipe Earl Grey pastry cream into the centre of the ring of chouquettes (*Photo G*).

15. Place the whipping cream, icing sugar, and vanilla in a stand mixer bowl. Whip on medium-high speed until medium peaks form.

16. Fill the piping bag fitted with the St. Honoré tip or a star tip of your choice with whipped cream and pipe a decorative mound on top of the pastry cream (*Photo H*).

STORAGE · The St. Honoré is best served the day it's assembled. It will keep in the refrigerator for up to two days, but be aware that the pastry will progressively soften.

MILLE-FEUILLES
des RÊVES

When I was a little girl, the dessert that held me most in awe was the vanilla mille-feuille (sometimes referred to as Napoleon slice or vanilla slice) purveyed by our neighbourhood bakery. I would go there and stare hungrily at the intricate patterned icing on the top and the custard sandwiched between flaky layers of pastry. Today, our Mille-feuille des Rêves—'thousand (pastry) layers of my dreams'—showcases a delectable combination of raspberry, passionfruit, and coconut. A dream come true! This dessert is best eaten the day it's assembled but you can make most of its elements ahead of time and have them ready for assembling the day you plan on serving it. The puff pastry can be made well in advance, kept frozen, and baked as needed.

EQUIPMENT · You will need a stand mixer fitted with a whisk attachment and two piping bags, one of them fitted with a medium round tip (#803 or #804).

ASSEMBLY

1 × 11-by-15-inch sheet	Puff Pastry, baked and caramelized (*page 244*)
1 batch	Coconut Buttercream (*page 33*)
20 g (¼ cup)	shredded coconut
½ pint (1 cup)	fresh raspberries
	icing sugar, for finishing

PASSION CREAM

3	large egg yolks
2	large eggs
70 g (¼ cup + 2 Tbsp)	sugar
200 g (¾ cup)	passionfruit purée (*see 'Fruit Purées,' page 19*)
113 g (½ cup)	unsalted butter, cold

TO MAKE THE PASSION CREAM

1. Place the egg yolks, eggs, and sugar in a stand mixer bowl. With a whisk attachment, whip the mixture on medium-high speed for about 5 minutes, until the eggs reach the ribbon stage. They should be thick and pale.

2. While your eggs are whipping, scald the passion-fruit purée in a small saucepan.

3. When your eggs have reached the ribbon stage, turn the mixer down to low and slowly pour in the scalded purée. If you add the hot purée too quickly the eggs will curdle and your passion cream will come out lumpy. Transfer the warm mixture back into the saucepan.

4. Over medium-low heat and whisking constantly, bring the mixture to a boil and cook for 2 minutes.

5. Remove from heat. Immediately strain the passion cream through a fine mesh strainer to remove any lumps. Add the butter and whisk until smooth; or, if you want your cream even smoother, use an immersion blender.

6. Transfer the passion cream to a bowl, cover, and refrigerate for 2 to 3 hours, until set.

CONTINUED

7. Using a sharp serrated knife, trim the edges of the puff pastry sheet to create straight edges (no more than a few centimetres on each side). Using a ruler as a guide, cut the sheet into 12 equal pieces (*Photo A*).

8. Toast the shredded coconut in an oven at 350°F (180°C) for 8 to 10 minutes, until golden brown. Set aside to cool.

9. Fill the piping bag fitted with the tip with coconut buttercream.

10. Each of the mille-feuilles will require 3 layers of puff pastry. On the bottom layer, pipe 10 dots of coconut buttercream (*Photo B*) and sprinkle with toasted coconut.

11. Gently place a second layer of pastry on top of the coconut buttercream. Slice 12 raspberries in half and arrange 6 halves around the edges of each rectangle (*Photo C*).

12. Fill the piping bag with no tip with passion cream, cut the end off, and pipe cream between the raspberries (*Photo D*).

13. Using a piece of parchment paper as a mask, dust the remaining pieces of pastry with icing sugar (*Photo E*) and place on top of the raspberries and passion cream (*Photo F*). Pipe a dot of passion cream on top and garnish with a raspberry. Let the mille-feuilles rest in the refrigerator for a few hours before serving.

STORAGE · These mille-feuilles will keep in the refrigerator for two days, but be aware that the pastry will progressively soften.

SWEETs

Working with CHOCOLATE

Chocolate is one of my favourite ingredients to work with in the kitchen. Whether making chocolate garnishes or stirring it with cream to make a silky smooth ganache, I find the process very satisfying. Chocolate isn't as difficult to work with as you might think. In this section I explain the basics of working with chocolate and provide you with three recipes for chocolate garnishes to give your desserts and pastries that extra boost of sophistication.

BUYING CHOCOLATE · Chocolate comes in many forms: little buttons called callets, chips, bricks, or bars. Callets are practical because they melt down so easily; larger pieces should be chopped up smaller before being melted.

Always use good quality chocolate for all your baking. At minimum, that means chocolate that has been made with cocoa butter: that's what gives great chocolate its beautiful texture and flavour. In lower quality chocolate, where cocoa butter is replaced with cheaper vegetable oils or fats, these qualities are sacrificed.

For almost all of our kitchen's chocolate needs, our preferred brand is Valrhona, which we also sell in our Provisions store and our online shop. Other excellent brands that are easy to find are Callebaut and Cacao Barry. A bit of research will yield many more possibilities.

MELTING CHOCOLATE · Melting chocolate is a very simple process. The easiest way of going about it is to use a double boiler. Fill a small saucepan halfway with water and place it over medium heat. Find a bowl that fits securely on the rim of the saucepan without touching the water. Put your chocolate pieces in the bowl and stir occasionally until completely melted. If water starts to sputter out from beneath the bowl, turn the heat down to reduce the boil.

Chocolate can be melted in the microwave. In order to avoid burning it, make sure you run your microwave on half power in short spurts, stirring at each interval, until the chocolate is melted.

STORING CHOCOLATE · Never store your chocolate in the refrigerator or freezer. Moisture is chocolate's enemy and in those environments, water condensation will cause the sugar to bloom. Instead, wrap your chocolate well and keep it in a dry, dark place. That will ensure that its aromas and flavours stay preserved.

TEMPERING CHOCOLATE · When chocolate is melted down with the specific purpose of hardening it into a new shape, it needs to be tempered. The chocolate you buy was tempered in order to get it into its shape (callets, bars, etc.). You can tell because it's shiny, has a nice snap when you cut it or bite into it, is smooth when you taste it, and doesn't melt all over your fingers right away. All of these qualities come from the cocoa butter in the chocolate.

When you melt chocolate, its great qualities melt away with it as the cocoa butter becomes unstable. If you let it set again without tempering it, it will take a long time to set, become grainy, develop large and unattractive streaks or spots, and melt to the touch. In order to restore the chocolate's good qualities, you must re-temper it, which means—put very simply—restabilizing the cocoa butter by controlling its temperature.

Although it might sound scary, tempering is actually pretty straightforward. Entire books have been dedicated to working with chocolate, but for your purposes as a home baker you really only need to master the one simple tempering method I have outlined on page 261. You can use it to make the sweets we present over the following pages: chocolate garnishes, almond toffee rochers, and my favourite—mendiants.

TIPS & TRICKS FOR
tempering chocolate

— Follow the recipe as closely as possible.

— Use an instant-read digital thermometer.

— In order for your chocolate to set, make sure it's not too warm in your kitchen.

— Use the best quality chocolate that you can find.

— Work with the chocolate as soon as it's tempered. If you leave it for too long, it will begin to harden and become difficult to work with.

— You can always re-warm your chocolate to the final temperature if it's cooling too quickly, but be careful not to go above 32°C (90°F) or you will have to start the tempering process all over again. You can test your chocolate by spreading a small amount on a plate. It should set within 5 to 7 minutes, without any visible streaks.

— When preparing the water bath use cold tap water. With such a small quantity of chocolate, an ice bath will cool down your chocolate too quickly.

— If you make a mistake with temperatures during the tempering process, that's OK—you can always melt it down and try again. There is never any need to throw away chocolate!

— It's very important not to let any water get into the chocolate: even one drop will cause it to seize and render it unusable for tempering. To prevent this from happening, after you're finished with the double boiler and water bath, wipe down the outside of the chocolate bowl to avoid water dripping on your tray or work surface. If water does get into the chocolate, just save it for a recipe where the chocolate doesn't need to be tempered, such as a ganache, chocolate cake, or brownies.

— Even though the garnish recipes we provide on the following pages require only 140 g (1 cup) of chocolate, our tempering method calls for 280 g (2 cups) because any amount smaller than this is really difficult to work with. Simply spread the leftover chocolate on a piece of parchment paper, set it aside to harden, chop it up, and save it for any recipe calling for chocolate in the future.

HOW TO TEMPER
· *chocolate* ·

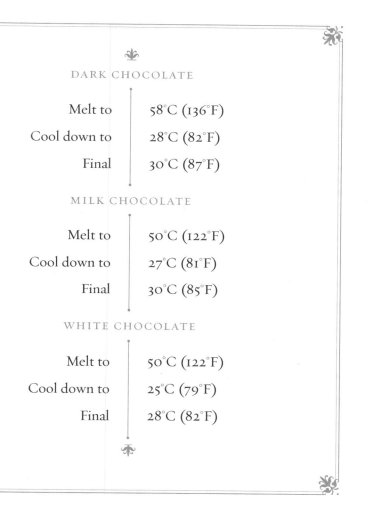

DARK CHOCOLATE

Melt to	58°C (136°F)
Cool down to	28°C (82°F)
Final	30°C (87°F)

MILK CHOCOLATE

Melt to	50°C (122°F)
Cool down to	27°C (81°F)
Final	30°C (85°F)

WHITE CHOCOLATE

Melt to	50°C (122°F)
Cool down to	25°C (79°F)
Final	28°C (82°F)

Tempering involves heating the chocolate to a certain temperature, cooling it down to a second temperature, and bringing it back up to a final temperature. These temperatures vary according to the type of chocolate being used (dark, milk, or white) and the brand of chocolate.

The table of temperatures to the left is for each of the three types of Valrhona chocolate. If you're using a different brand of chocolate, refer to the packaging or their website for the correct temperatures.

EQUIPMENT · You will need an instant-read digital thermometer.

PROCEDURE

1. Weigh out 280 g chocolate in a bowl.

2. Bring a small saucepan of water to a boil and remove from heat. Place the bowl of chocolate over the saucepan to create a double boiler and let the chocolate melt slowly until it reaches the appropriate melting temperature as indicated in the table. Remove the bowl of chocolate from the saucepan and set the saucepan aside, reserving the hot water for step 5.

3. Set the bowl of chocolate inside a large bowl filled with just enough cold tap water to reach a quarter of the way up the sides of the bowl of chocolate. The bowl should not be floating; it should be stable enough for you to comfortably stir the chocolate.

4. Stir constantly, scraping down the sides of the bowl, until the temperature of the chocolate has dropped to its cooling temperature as indicated in the table. Remove the bowl from the cold water bath.

5. Set the bowl back over the pot of hot water. Stir until the temperature has gone back up to within a couple degrees of its final temperature as indicated in the table. Remove the bowl from the pot and stir the chocolate vigorously for 30 seconds. The temperature will continue to rise after you've removed it from the heat, so check the temperature one final time after stirring to make sure it hasn't gone back above 32°C (90°F) (if it has, you will need to start the tempering process over). Your chocolate is now tempered and must be used immediately.

Salted
CHOCOLATE BARK

This salted chocolate bark recipe can be garnished with a wide variety of flavours. Some of our favourites include feuilletine (caramelized cereal flakes), toasted coconut, crushed pistachio, and dried fruit powders. This simple garnish will add an elegant finishing touch to desserts. Please note: you will only need half the amount of chocolate that you tempered to make this garnish.

PROCEDURE · Line a baking sheet with parchment paper.

1. Pour the tempered chocolate onto the parchment paper and, using an offset spatula, spread it out *(Photo A)*. Gently tap the tray on the counter to even it out.

2. Sprinkle the chocolate with fleur de sel and a garnish of your choice *(Photo B)*.

3. Once the chocolate has set, break into shards *(Photo C)*.

STORAGE · This garnish will keep in a cool, dry place for up to three weeks. Do not refrigerate.

CHOCOLATE
cigarettes

To make chocolate cigarettes, your chocolate needs to be starting to set but still soft. If it's too hard, it will break into pieces when you try to scrape it and if it's too soft, it won't roll nicely. This leaves you quite a small window of time to work with, but with practice, you'll soon get a feel for it. Please note: you will only need half the amount of chocolate that you tempered to make this garnish.

EQUIPMENT · You will need a large metal scraper. You can use a kitchen scraper designed for working with dough or an inexpensive bench scraper from the paint section at your local hardware store. You will also need a work surface. A piece of marble or granite is best as the scraper can damage your counter. Offcuts can be purchased from local suppliers at reasonable prices.

PROCEDURE

1. Pour the tempered chocolate onto your clean work surface. Using an offset spatula, spread the chocolate in a long strip 6 to 7 inches wide (*Photo A*).

2. When your chocolate just starts to set, use the metal scraper to create straight edges on both sides of the chocolate (*Photo B*). Make sure that the width of the chocolate strip ends up narrower than the width of your scraper.

3. Firmly grip the scraper with both hands. Angle it at about 45 degrees with the work surface and measure out about ½ inch of chocolate. Push down and forward in one swift motion to cut off a cigarette (*Photo C*). The chocolate will roll itself up tightly. Repeat until all the chocolate is used up.

STORAGE · This garnish will keep in a cool, dry place for up to three weeks. Do not refrigerate.

white chocolate PETALS

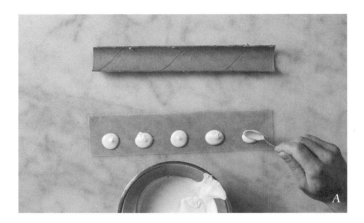

Please note: you will only need half the amount of chocolate that you tempered to make this garnish.

EQUIPMENT · You will need a cardboard tube.

PROCEDURE

1. Cut a cardboard tube in half along its length. Prepare a few pieces of parchment paper about 3 by 12 inches in size. You will form the white chocolate petals in batches, working with one piece of parchment paper at a time.

2. Drop spoonfuls of tempered white chocolate along a piece of parchment paper in small mounds about 2 inches apart (*Photo A*).

3. Using the back of the spoon, spread each mound of chocolate away from you to create a petal shape. Repeat for all mounds (*Photo B*). Immediately position the strip of parchment paper inside the curved tube (*Photo C*).

4. Repeat steps 2 and 3 until you have the desired amount of petals.

5. When the chocolate is set, gently peel the petals off the parchment paper (*Photo D*).

STORAGE · This garnish will keep in a cool, dry place for up to three weeks. Do not refrigerate.

DUCHESS
hot chocolate mix

MAKES 2¼ CUPS MIX

Nothing beats a cup of hot chocolate on a cold winter's day, especially when it features well-chosen spices. Make sure you use the best quality chocolate you can find to really seal the deal. If you have leftover chocolate from tempering or other recipes this is a great way to use it up.

INGREDIENT NOTES · We use Valrhona 66% Caraïbe callets for the dark chocolate, Valrhona 40% Jivara callets for the milk chocolate, and Valrhona cocoa powder.

PROCEDURE · Put all the ingredients in a food processor and pulse until the large chunks have disappeared. It's fine if a few chunks remain. If you don't have a food processor, chop the chocolate finely by hand. Mix with the remaining ingredients.

TO SERVE · Put 4 Tbsp hot chocolate mix in a mug. Slowly pour in 1 cup hot milk, stirring constantly until the chocolate has dissolved.

STORAGE · This hot chocolate mix will keep for up to six months in a well-sealed container stored in a cool, dry place.

INGREDIENTS

175 g (1¼ cups)	dark chocolate
100 g (¾ cup)	milk chocolate
30 g (¼ cup)	cocoa powder
3 Tbsp	sugar
¼ tsp	ground nutmeg
¼ tsp	ground allspice
pinch	ground cardamom
pinch	salt

Mendiants

INGREDIENTS

280 g (2 cups)	dark chocolate (*see headnote*)
¼ cup	unsalted pistachios
¼ cup	dried cherries
¼ cup	small pieces ribboned coconut, or shredded coconut
	fleur de sel

Mendiants are a traditional French chocolate confection meant to symbolize the mendicant monastic orders. Traditionally each chocolate disk would feature a particular nut or type of fruit to symbolize each of the orders, but nowadays mendiants come with all kinds of different combinations of nuts, dried fruit, fruit peel, fruit powders, and spices.

For us, a mendiant is really about showcasing the chocolate it's made of. Our favourite chocolates to use are Valrhona 64% Manjari, which has fresh, acidic, and fruit undertones, and Valrhona 67% Ashanti, with its hints of licorice, hazelnut, cinnamon, and tonka bean. Go ahead and top the mendiants with whatever fruits or nuts strike your fancy, but try to keep it simple to really allow the chocolate's flavours to shine through.

INGREDIENT NOTES · The tempering temperatures given in this recipe are for Valrhona dark chocolate callets. If you're using a different brand of chocolate, refer to the packaging or their website for the correct tempering temperatures.

EQUIPMENT · You will need two baking sheets, a piping bag, and an instant-read digital thermometer.

TO TEMPER THE CHOCOLATE · Line the baking sheets with parchment paper (*see page 259 for a discussion on tempering chococlate*).

I. Bring a small saucepan of water to a boil and remove from heat. Place the chocolate in a bowl over the saucepan to create a double boiler and let the chocolate melt slowly until it reaches 58°C (136°F). Remove the bowl of chocolate from the saucepan and set the saucepan aside, reserving the hot water for step 4.

CONTINUED

2. Set the bowl of chocolate over a large bowl filled with just enough cold tap water to reach about a quarter of the way up the sides of the bowl of chocolate. The bowl should not be floating: it needs to be stable enough for you to comfortably stir the chocolate.

3. Stir constantly, scraping down the sides of the bowl, until the temperature of the chocolate has dropped to 28°C (82°F). Remove the bowl from the cold water bath.

4. Set the bowl back over the pot of hot water. Stir until the temperature has gone back up to 30°C (87°F). Remove the bowl from the pot and stir vigorously for 30 seconds. Your chocolate is now tempered and must be used immediately.

5. Pour half of the chocolate onto a lined baking sheet and spread it out using an offset spatula. Set it aside to harden, then chop it up and save it for a future purpose.

TO FORM THE MENDIANTS

6. Fill a piping bag with the remaining tempered chocolate. Cut a small hole at the bottom of the bag and pipe small chocolate circles about 1 inch in diameter onto a lined baking sheet (*Photo A*).

7. In the centre of each circle, gently place a pistachio, a dried cherry, and a coconut ribbon or a sprinkling of shredded coconut (*Photo B*). Sprinkle lightly with fleur de sel.

8. Leave the mendiants to set in a cool, dry place.

STORAGE · Mendiants will keep in a cool, dry place for up to two weeks. Do not refrigerate.

ALMOND *TOFFEE* ROCHERS

MAKES 24 ROCHERS

These chocolate bites are highly addictive. Unlike chocolate haystacks, which are made with coconut, rochers feature crunchy toffee and almond bits for that added decadence. They make a wonderful present around the holidays, so be sure to make plenty to give your family and friends.

INGREDIENT NOTES · For the dark chocolate we use Valrhona 66% Caraïbe callets. The tempering temperatures listed below are for Valrhona dark chocolate callets. If you're using a different brand of chocolate, refer to the packaging or their website for the correct tempering temperatures.

EQUIPMENT · You will need an instant-read digital thermometer and two baking sheets lined with parchment paper.

TO PREPARE THE TOFFEE AND ALMONDS

1. Place the butter, sugar, water, and salt in a saucepan. Cook over medium heat, stirring occasionally, until the temperature reaches 146°C (295°F) or the colour is golden brown. Once the mixture starts to darken, the temperature will rise quite quickly, so keep a constant eye on it and be ready to take it off the heat as soon as it reaches the right temperature or colour.

INGREDIENTS

113 g (½ cup)	unsalted butter
112 g (½ cup + 1 Tbsp)	sugar
1 Tbsp	water
¼ tsp	salt
1 tsp	vanilla extract or paste
192 g (1½ cups)	slivered almonds
280 g (2 cups)	dark chocolate

CONTINUED

2. Remove from heat and stir in the vanilla.

3. Immediately pour the toffee out onto a lined baking sheet. Using an offset spatula, spread it out thinly. Allow to cool and harden completely.

4. Using a paper towel, blot any excess oil that may have appeared on the toffee. Crush the toffee into small pieces and slivers. Set the slivers aside and re-line the baking sheet.

5. Preheat your oven to 350°F (180°C). Spread the slivered almonds on the lined baking sheet and toast for 10 to 12 minutes, until they are light brown. Set aside to cool.

TO TEMPER THE CHOCOLATE · Make sure both the almonds and toffee are completely cool before you start to temper your chocolate (*see page 259 for a discussion on tempering chocolate*).

6. Bring a small saucepan of water to a boil and remove from heat. Place the bowl of chocolate over the saucepan to create a double boiler and let the chocolate melt slowly until it reaches 58°C (136°F). Remove the bowl of chocolate from the saucepan and set the saucepan aside, reserving the hot water for step 9.

7. Set the bowl of chocolate inside a large bowl filled with just enough cold tap water to reach about a quarter of the way up the sides of the bowl of chocolate. The bowl should not be floating: it needs to be stable enough for you to comfortably stir the chocolate.

8. Stir constantly, scraping down the sides of the bowl, until the temperature of the chocolate has dropped to 28°C (82°F). Remove the bowl from the cold water bath.

9. Set the bowl back over the pot of hot water. Stir until the temperature has gone back up to 30°C (87°F). Remove the bowl from the pot and stir the chocolate vigorously for 30 seconds. Your chocolate is now tempered and must be used immediately.

TO MAKE THE ROCHERS

10. As soon as the chocolate is tempered, transfer the toffee pieces and slivered almonds into a larger bowl. Pour in about half the tempered chocolate and mix everything together.

11. Using a small ice cream scoop or a spoon, scoop rochers onto a lined baking sheet. Set aside to harden.

12. Re-line the other baking sheet. Pour the remaining chocolate onto it and spread it out using an offset spatula. After it has hardened, chop it up and save it for a future purpose.

STORAGE · These rochers will keep in a cool, dry place for up to two weeks. Do not refrigerate.

Making a
CARAMEL

Working with sugar and caramel can be a little daunting at first, but practice makes perfect. I hope that this section will help increase your confidence in cooking sugar.

The basic method for cooking sugar involves heating or boiling it until it reaches the right stage for your recipe, which means either a specific temperature or a desired colour. Sometimes additional liquids are added at the end of the cooking.

There are two main ways to cook sugar: in combination with water or dry. In this section I break down both these processes for you.

COOKING SUGAR WITH WATER · When sugar is cooked in combination with water, as the mixture boils, the water evaporates while the sugar slowly cooks, darkens, and turns into a caramel. Usually when making a caramel we judge that it's done when it has reached an amber colour. After your sugar has started to boil, it will start to turn slightly golden. At that point the caramelization process will start to happen very quickly, so keep a close eye on it. When you see a honey colour, you are very close. The caramel will then take on a nice amber colour, at which point it's ready. Immediately take it off the heat and proceed to any additional steps to finish it. The more colour on the caramel, the more flavour—but be aware that the line between just done and burnt is very fine!

Often you will be adding additional liquids to your caramel after it's reached colour, such as juice or cream. If this is the case, it's important to use a good-sized saucepan as the sugar will bubble up a lot when the liquid is added. This phenomenon is amplified if the liquid you are adding is cold because of the wide difference in temperature. Adding cold liquid will also cause your sugar to seize up, and then it's difficult to get it perfectly smooth again. This is why we always heat or scald the liquids: it brings them closer to the temperature of the sugar and everything combines better.

Have your liquid heated before your sugar is ready because once it gets its amber shade, you won't have much time before it overcooks. Take it off the heat and add the liquid very slowly and in small increments. As you add it, stir the caramel constantly using a wooden spoon or a heatproof spatula. The sugar will be extremely hot, so you might want to use an oven mitt to protect your hand from the steam. Some of the sugar may harden as the liquid is added, but if you keep stirring it should melt down, giving you a smooth caramel. If there are a few lumps that won't dissolve you can strain the finished caramel for a smooth texture.

Sometimes recipes call for sugar to be cooked to a specific temperature. For example, to make spiced nuts, the sugar is cooked to 117°C (242°F) and then the nuts are added. An instant-read digital thermometer is imperative in such recipes.

CONTINUED

COOKING SUGAR DRY · This method involves putting only sugar crystals in a saucepan to melt. The upside to this method is that the sugar cooks much faster and by the time it's completely melted, it's already reached that perfect amber colour and is ready for your liquid additions or to use in a recipe. The downside is that the sugar needs constant attention and can easily overcook, so you need to be watching the colour closely. That makes it a bit trickier.

For this method, weigh out the sugar and have it ready. Start with a clean saucepan, sprinkle in a layer of sugar, and put it over medium heat. It will take a few minutes for the sugar to start to melt, but once it does, it will melt very fast. When you see the sugar liquefying around the edges of the saucepan, use a wooden spoon or heatproof spatula to gently drag the liquid sugar into the middle to absorb the sugar that's not yet melted, disturbing it as little as possible. When the sugar has melted almost completely, add another layer of sugar and continue as before. Repeat until you have added your last layer of sugar. Now wait for the sugar to finish melting down and is a nice amber colour. As soon as that happens it's ready.

Lumps may form as you add the sugar. They should just melt down during the melting process. You can try to break up large ones with your wooden spoon or spatula, but do so very gently, and above all, avoid stirring. If a few stubborn lumps of sugar persist at the end of the melting process when your sugar is at colour, you can strain them out—after adding any liquid additions —to ensure a smooth caramel.

CRYSTALLIZATION · The main problem that can occur when making a caramel is crystallization. It's very obvious when sugar crystallizes: it lumps together, stops melting, turns opaque, and becomes a crumbly mass. If this happens, there is no saving it, and you will have to start again.

TIPS & TRICKS · Here are a few tips to help prevent your sugar from crystallizing.

- Your saucepan and utensils must be meticulously clean and free of any foreign material.

- Do not stir your sugar mixture while it's cooking as this will very quickly cause it to crystallize. This is a common mistake as it's very tempting to stir. If you feel the need to stir, give your saucepan a gentle shake or swirl instead, doing so carefully as the sugar will be very hot.

- When weighing out a recipe that combines sugar with water, put your water in the saucepan first, and then sprinkle the sugar on top. That way all the sugar gets absorbed and there are no dry spots left in the bottom of the saucepan. As it comes to a boil the sugar will dissolve and start to cook.

- We often include a little bit of corn syrup or glucose in our caramel recipes as their properties help prevent the sugar from crystallizing as it cooks.

SALTED CARAMEL

Salted caramel is the star of our most popular macaron and a bestseller sold in jars in our Provisions store. For a detailed discussion of caramel, see 'Making a Caramel' on pages 271–272.

INGREDIENTS

130 g (½ cup + 1 Tbsp)	whipping cream
270 g (1⅓ cups)	sugar
200 g (¾ cup + 2 Tbsp)	unsalted butter, cubed
30 g (¼ cup)	almond flour (finely ground almonds)
¾ tsp	fleur de sel or salt

PROCEDURE

1. Heat the cream in a microwave or a small saucepan on the stove until scalding. Set aside and try to keep hot as you melt the sugar.

2. Place about a quarter of the sugar in a wide-bottomed saucepan over medium heat. Gently melt the sugar, swirling the saucepan around as needed (*Photo A*). Do not stir. Once the sugar is almost melted, sprinkle another quarter of the sugar into the saucepan, swirling as needed. Repeat twice more until all the sugar is completely melted and has turned amber in colour (*Photo B*).

3. Remove from heat and slowly pour in the hot whipping cream (*Photo C*). Be sure to pour slowly as the mixture will bubble up. Using a heatproof spatula or spoon, mix the caramel until smooth (*Photo D*). Using a fine mesh strainer, immediately strain the caramel into a bowl.

4. Mix the butter, almond flour, and fleur de sel into the hot caramel until all the butter is melted and incorporated. To achieve an extra-smooth result, you may use an immersion blender. Transfer the caramel into jars or a container, let cool, and refrigerate until set.

STORAGE · Salted caramel will keep in the refrigerator for up to two weeks.

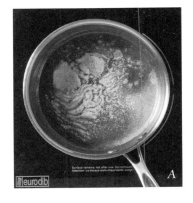

vanilla bean
MARSHMALLOWS

We are all familiar with roasting marshmallows at the campfire or floating them in a steaming cup of hot chocolate—but don't just leave it at that. Marshmallow can be a creative way to fill macarons, sandwich cookies, or use between cake layers. And they are so much easier to make than you think!

EQUIPMENT · You will need a stand mixer fitted with a whisk attachment, a 9-by-9-inch pan, and an instant-read digital thermometer.

PROCEDURE · Line the pan with parchment paper, creating 'handles' that hang over two opposing edges for lifting the marshmallow out of the pan after it's set. Lightly spray the pan and parchment paper with vegetable oil.

INGREDIENTS

85 g (⅓ cup)	ice water
21 g (2 Tbsp)	powdered gelatin
123 g (⅓ cup + 1 Tbsp)	white corn syrup
340 g (1¾ cups)	sugar
85 g (⅓ cup)	water
123 g (⅓ cup + 1 Tbsp)	white corn syrup
1 tsp	vanilla paste *or* seeds from 1 vanilla bean
	icing sugar, for covering and coating the marshmallows
	vegetable oil or cooking spray

1. Make sure the water is ice cold. Put the water in a small microwavable bowl, sprinkle the gelatin over, and stir to dissolve. Set aside at room temperature until firmly set.

2. In the bowl of a stand mixer fitted with a whisk attachment, place the first measure of corn syrup. Heat the gelatin in a microwave until melted, about 30 seconds, then add it to the corn syrup.

3. In a small saucepan, place the sugar, water, and second measure of corn syrup. Heat the mixture until it reaches a final temperature of between 112° and 115°C (235° and 240°F).

4. Turn the mixer on at low speed and gradually pour the cooked sugar down the side of the mixing bowl. Once all the sugar has been incorporated, turn the speed up to medium-high and mix for 5 minutes, or until the marshmallow looks stiff, light, and fluffy and is pulling away from the sides of the bowl. If you underwhip the marshmallow it will turn out dense rather than airy and soft.

5. Add the vanilla paste and mix on high for 1 minute. If adding other flavourings or extracts, do so at this point (*see 'Variations'*).

6. Pour the marshmallow into the prepared pan and, using a spatula coated in cooking spray, spread it evenly (*Photos B–C*). Remember to spray anything you are using to touch the marshmallow—it will stick to everything!

7. Sift icing sugar over the marshmallow to cover well. Let set at room temperature for at least 6 hours before cutting.

8. To cut the marshmallow, run a knife along the sides of the pan and, using the parchment handles, gently lift it out onto a cutting board. Sift more icing sugar into a small bowl. Using a wheel cutter or sharp knife coated in cooking spray, cut the marshmallow into 35 rectangular pieces (*Photo D*). Dip each piece individually in the icing sugar to coat completely.

STORAGE · Marshmallows will keep in an airtight container or plastic wrap at room temperature for up to two weeks. Wrap them well so they don't dry out.

VARIATIONS · At step 5, you can use 1 tsp extract or 1 Tbsp compound of your choice to change the flavour of your marshmallows. Be careful not to add too much extra liquid to this recipe as this could affect the texture of your marshmallows. Here are two of the popular flavours we make at Duchess.

– *Toasted Coconut*
Toast 180 g (2 cups) shredded coconut in an oven at 350°F (180°C) until golden brown. Add 1 Tbsp coconut compound or 1 tsp coconut extract to the marshmallow at step 5. Omit the icing sugar. Once spread in the pan, lightly cover the marshmallow with half the toasted coconut. Once the marshmallow is set and cut, roll the pieces in the remaining toasted coconut.

– *Fuzzy Peach*
At step 5, add 1 Tbsp peach compound. Omit the icing sugar. Mix together 4 g (1 tsp) citric acid and 200 g (1 cup) sugar. Once spread in the pan, lightly cover the marshmallow with half the sugar mixture. Once the marshmallow is set and cut, roll the pieces in the remaining sugar mixture.

SPICED
— NUTS

INGREDIENTS

1 Tbsp	cocoa butter
pinch	ground nutmeg
½ tsp	ground cinnamon
¼ tsp	fleur de sel or salt
pinch	ground black pepper
pinch	ground ginger
pinch	ground cloves
pinch	ground allspice
100 g (1 cup)	whole pecans
70 g (½ cup)	whole blanched and peeled almonds
60 g (½ cup)	whole blanched and peeled hazelnuts
75 g (¼ cup + 2 Tbsp)	sugar
2 Tbsp	water

We make these during the holiday season to sell on our retail wall. The only problem is that we never seem to get that many out there to sell because we end up eating most of them ourselves!

This recipe is flexible in terms of the type of nuts that can be used and the spice ratio, so go ahead and adjust these to your liking. Remember to use nuts that are fresh and haven't been sitting around in your cupboard in case they've gone rancid. If you can't find cocoa butter, unsalted butter will work, but that will decrease the shelf life to about two weeks.

EQUIPMENT · You will need a small baking sheet and an instant-read digital thermometer.

PROCEDURE · Preheat your oven to 350°F (180°C).

1. Slowly melt the cocoa butter in a microwave. Add the spices and mix until well combined.

2. Place the nuts on a baking sheet and heat them in the oven until warmed, about 5 minutes. Keep them warm while you cook the sugar.

3. In a small saucepan just large enough to hold the nuts, combine the sugar and water and cook over medium heat until the mixture reaches 117°C (242°F).

4. Make sure the nuts are warm, and then add them to the cooked sugar (if the nuts aren't warm enough the sugar will seize) (*Photo A*). Stir with a wooden spoon until the sugar has crystallized on the nuts (*Photos B–C*). They will look dry and white.

5. Transfer the nuts to a larger saucepan placed over low heat. Stir constantly until caramelized (*Photo D*). If the nuts seem to be caramelizing too quickly, remove from heat briefly while continuing to stir. The nuts are done when they are shiny and dark caramel in colour.

6. Remove from heat and add the cocoa butter and spices, stirring until the nuts are coated (*Photo E*). Immediately pour the hot nuts onto a baking sheet and separate them out with a wooden spoon to prevent them from sticking together (*Photo F*). The nuts will be very hot at this point so be careful not to touch them.

7. Once the nuts are cool, you can break up any large chunks with your hands.

STORAGE · These nuts will keep in a cool, dry place for up to one month.

raspberry
ROSE JAM

This is my favourite jam to eat on warm brioche in the morning. At Duchess, it features as a layer in our Duchess cake. I prefer my jam 'à la française'—that is, looser and relying on the fruit's natural pectin to set it. This jam fits the bill. It will always remind me of my first trip to Alsace where I tasted the perfect raspberry jam.

Whether you like your raspberry jam with seeds or without is a matter of taste. I fall in the middle, so I discard half the seeds. Your choice!

INGREDIENTS

1 kg (about 6 cups)	fresh or frozen raspberries
900 g (4½ cups)	sugar
3 Tbsp	freshly squeezed lemon juice
1½ Tbsp	rose water

EQUIPMENT · You will need an instant-read digital thermometer, a water bath canner, and 3 × 250-ml canning jars with the appropriate seals.

PROCEDURE · Sanitize the jars and seals for 5 minutes in the water bath canner before starting to make the jam.

1. Combine the raspberries, sugar, and lemon juice in a saucepan. Bring to a simmer over medium-low heat, stirring frequently with a heatproof spatula or a wooden spoon.

2. Once the raspberries have begun to break down, remove from heat. Run half the mixture through a food mill or push it through a fine mesh strainer to remove the seeds. Discard the seeds and add the strained mixture back to the saucepan.

3. Bring the jam to a boil over medium heat. Cook until it reaches a temperature of 105°C (221°F), stirring frequently and carefully skimming off any foam collecting around the edges of the saucepan.

4. When the jam reaches temperature, remove from heat and immediately stir in the rose water.

5. Pour into the canning jars, seal well, and process in a water bath canner for 5 minutes.

STORAGE · Unopened jars of jam will keep in a cool, dry place for up to six months. Store opened jars in the refrigerator for up to one month.

Apple EARL GREY Jelly

INGREDIENTS

1.5 kg (7 or 8 medium)	Granny Smith apples
1.5 kg (6¼ cups)	water
3 Tbsp	lemon juice
1 kg (5 cups)	sugar
200 g (¾ cup + 1 Tbsp)	water
30 g	loose Earl Grey tea
about 1 tsp	finely ground Earl Grey tea (a pinch per jar)

EQUIPMENT · You will need cheesecloth, an instant-read digital thermometer, a blender (or immersion blender), a water bath canner, and 5 × 250-ml canning jars with the appropriate seals.

PROCEDURE

1. Stem and quarter the apples. Place them in a large pot on high heat with the 1.5 kg (6¼ cups) measure of water. When the water comes to a boil, turn the heat down to low and let it simmer for about 30 minutes, or until the apples are soft and pulpy. Remove from heat and blend.

2. Wet a large piece of double-layered cheesecloth. Fill it with the cooked apples, tie it off, and find a way to hang it over a large bowl or container. Allow the juice to strain out overnight.

3. The next day, sanitize the jars and seals for 5 minutes in a water bath canner and set aside.

4. Measure out 1 kg of strained apple juice, taking care to leave the sediment at the bottom of the container. Place the apple juice in a saucepan with the lemon juice and sugar. Boil for 8 minutes without stirring, carefully skimming off any foam.

5. While the jelly is cooking, bring the 200 g (¾ cup + 1 Tbsp) measure of water to a boil. Remove from heat and add the loose tea. Let steep for 3 minutes, strain, and set aside.

6. Also while the jelly is cooking, place a pinch of ground tea into the bottom of each jar.

7. Once the jelly has boiled for 8 minutes, add the steeped tea and continue to boil, without stirring, until the temperature reaches between 104° and 105°C (219° and 221°F). Skim off foam as needed.

8. When the jelly reaches temperature, immediately pour it into the canning jars, seal well, and process in a water bath canner for 5 minutes.

STORAGE · Unopened jars of apple jelly will keep for up to six months when stored in a cool, dry place. Store opened jars in the refrigerator for up to one month.

ACKNOWLEDGEMENTS

This book is the culmination of over five years of hard work and the efforts of a huge number of people. While we can't thank everybody individually please know we are immensely grateful to all who have helped us in this journey. We would like to thank Sarah Hervieux and Sarah Ares for all of their hard work and dedication to this project. All the fiddling with forks and flowers was worth it and we appreciate your attention to detail and dedication to making our products look their best. Thank you to the very best editor (and sister) Mona-Lynn Courteau for keeping us on pace, thinking about the small details, and asking the tough questions. And thank you to Giselle and Jacob's moms Sylvia Courteau and Cindy Pelletier as well as all of our other recipe testers for their invaluable feedback.

For the blind faith and undying support that our families have given us, we are eternally grateful. Thank you to Sarah Gallagher for keeping the kitchen running smoothly, allowing Jacob the time off to perfect the recipes in this book. To all of our staff, both past and present and to whom this book is dedicated, we are sincerely grateful for all of your hard work. Finally, we would like to thank Mitchell Parsons for having faith in us and giving us a chance to pursue our dream of opening a bake shop.

PROVISIONS by DUCHESS

When I started baking seriously at home and challenging myself with more difficult recipes, my biggest obstacle was finding the ingredients and tools I needed. Provisions by Duchess, our shop next to the bakery and our online store, is a place where home bakers, pastry chefs, and professionals alike can come to find everything in one place. We offer the finest available in dry goods, extracts, compounds, preserves, and tools—everything you need to create the recipes in this book! We hope you will leave feeling inspired to try new things at home.

Some of the trusted ingredients we carry are Valrhona and Callebaut chocolate, almond flour, organic milled flours, freeze-dried fruit, and 84% butter. We also carry a full line of anodized aluminum bakeware, piping tips, and a wide variety of specialty tools imported from France.

10720–124TH STREET, EDMONTON, AB T5M 0H1
WWW.DUCHESSPROVISIONS.COM